3—

A CRITICAL INTRODUCTION
TO THE GOSPELS

By the same Author

A CRITICAL INTRODUCTION
TO THE GOSPELS

BY

H. A. GUY, B.D., B.A.
Taunton's School, Southampton

LONDON

MACMILLAN & CO LTD

NEW YORK · ST MARTIN'S PRESS

1955

MACMILLAN AND COMPANY LIMITED
London Bombay Calcutta Madras Melbourne

THE MACMILLAN COMPANY OF CANADA LIMITED
Toronto

ST MARTIN'S PRESS INC
New York

PRINTED IN GREAT BRITAIN

PREFACE

This book is intended for two classes of readers. First, it is for the general reader who is interested in the study of the Gospels and the New Testament. He may have read or heard references to such matters as Form Criticism, "Q", Proto-Luke or the Johannine problem, and would like to know more about them but is afraid of tackling a long technical theological work. He will find here a summary and discussion of the views of modern scholars on such topics. It is hoped that this will assist him to understand the nature of the Gospels and to appreciate their contents and message. It may help to dispel some of the ignorance which is rife—both among those who accept and those who reject the Christian message—about the origins and character of the Gospels and their relations to each other.

The book is intended also for candidates for examinations. Most of the syllabuses for examinations on the New Testament, issued by university and other bodies, contain a section dealing with questions of the date, authorship and composition of the Gospels. This applies to examinations ranging from the General Certificate of Education (Advanced level) to certificates and diplomas in theology and even to degrees in Divinity. This book contains sufficient material for such candidates to be able to write in some detail on these matters.

It is essential that those who would seriously study this subject (especially those with an examination in

v

view) should read thoroughly and carefully, mastering each point as it is explained, preferably making their own outline of the argument, and should look up every reference which is made to the New Testament. There are far too many people—including examination candidates—who can talk in general terms about the Gospels and even argue vehemently for a particular point of view but are unable to support what they say by references to actual passages or quotations. A book such as this is used only superficially if it is taken as a substitute for close and detailed study of the Gospels themselves.

For both these classes of readers, a list of books for further study is given at the end. The contents of this book are based on the discussions and conclusions in these larger works. It will have fulfilled its function if it leads the reader to further study of some of these.

It will be readily seen that the author owes much to the larger standard works on the subject. To have acknowledged his debt for every statement made would have resulted in burdening the pages with numerous footnotes. In many cases it is impossible to state definitely the origin of an idea with which one has been familiar for years. He would like, however, to mention one publication which has been continually by his side, especially in writing chapters III to VI—Allan Barr's *Diagram of Synoptic Relations*. The reader will find this invaluable for reference and discover that close study of it will be a fascinating pursuit.

CONTENTS

CHAPTER I

CRITICISM OF THE GOSPELS

The word 'criticism', as popularly used, often conveys an impression quite different from its original and true meaning. To many people the term implies fault-finding and there are those who, hearing about critical work on the Bible or about critics of the Gospels, indignantly ask: What right have we to find fault with such books? If, however, the term is used correctly and is understood, no such intention is implied.

The words 'critic' and 'criticism' come from the Greek word *kritēs*, meaning a judge. Criticism means the careful and systematic study of a subject by one who is qualified to judge. Thus the dramatic critic of a newspaper is one who is able to give his considered judgment on plays and the theatre. The art critic gives his opinion but he must himself have made a study of the subject. The literary critic must have knowledge of many types of literature, so that he can guide the reading of people who have not made this their special study. Similarly the critic of the Bible is one who knows its books and their contents and is also acquainted with the views of other people about them. On this basis he is able to proceed to further study of the Bible and to help others along the same path.

Criticism of this kind does not mean fault-finding. It should in many cases rather be termed appreciation. It is the scientific study or judgment of a literary or other work. There are two requirements of such criticism. First, it must be real study; the critic must not indulge in merely superficial reading or accept the opinions of other people without investigation. Second, it must be thorough and impartial—in a word, 'scientific'. The critic must be prepared to weigh the different views which he meets, to consider various possibilities and theories. It is fatal for him to begin his study with his mind already made up. He must proceed from one stage to another, basing his conclusions on real evidence carefully weighed. He may find in the course of his study that he has to discard some of his previous ideas, but if he is honest he will see that this is necessary in order to arrive at an intelligent understanding of the work before him.

In the study of literature, two kinds of criticism have to be distinguished, Textual (or Lower) Criticism and Source (or Higher) Criticism.

TEXTUAL CRITICISM

This is the study of the 'text' of a book, an attempt to discover the original words as written by the author. In the case of books composed and printed in modern times, this is comparatively easy. We may have access to the original manuscript and in any case we can refer to the first printed edition. But when we come to study books which were produced before the invention of printing (i.e. all writings before the end of the fifteenth century), we have to rely on written copies or manuscripts (MSS.). This applies equally, to take a few examples at random, to the Anglo-Saxon Chronicle, the Domesday Book, the Confessions of St.

Augustine, the Gospels, the poetry of Virgil, the commentaries of Julius Caesar and the poems of Homer. The first copy of a book written by hand soon perishes. In no case have we the original MS. of any classical writer, whether Horace, Livy, Paul or Mark. We have to rely on copies made by scribes.

It is obviously too much to expect that scribes will always copy exactly, without making any mistakes or alterations. Hence there arise 'variants' or 'various readings'. Sometimes these consist of one word only or even one letter, but occasionally they differ to the extent of a whole phrase or sentence. Thus in the second book of Virgil's *Aeneid* there is a passage of twenty-two lines which was probably not written by Virgil, at least in that place. Some MSS. include them while others omit them. There are variants in the texts of all classical authors. This is also true of such a recent writer as Shakespeare. Early editions of his plays do not always agree in wording. Where we have not the actual MS. of Shakespeare himself, scholars have to weigh the evidence, considering various probabilities, to try to find out what Shakespeare wrote.

In the case of the New Testament books likewise there are variants in the MSS. The Christian scribe would probably be more careful in copying a Gospel or an Epistle than would the scribe of some Greek or Latin historian or poet. On the other hand, the Christian scribe, not being a professional, was probably, at least in the early centuries, not so proficient at his task. It was inevitable that, however careful and conscientious he might be, he was likely to make some mistakes; his eyes must often have been strained as he wrote and his hand must have got tired.

The errors made by a scribe fall into various types. Sometimes he would omit a word or a phrase or a whole line; this was particularly easy if the line ended with the same word as the previous line in the MS. Sometimes he inadvertently repeated a word or a line or mistook one letter for another. Certain Greek words were generally abbreviated in writing and a special mark was made to indicate that an abbreviation was being used. If the mark were omitted the scribe might take the word to be a different one, and this might give the sentence a quite different meaning. If the scribe found out his mistake afterwards, or if another did so, a correction could be inserted in the margin. A scribe might remember in one place that another MS. which he had seen had a different reading from the one which he was copying and he would put the alternative in the margin. Sometimes he had two or more MSS. in front of him and he would have to make a choice between them. He might produce a 'conflate' reading, by incorporating phrases from more than one MS.

In addition to these variants, largely unintentional on the part of scribes, they occasionally deliberately altered the text of the MS. before them. The scribe might do this in order to make a passage run more smoothly or to correct the grammar if he thought it was faulty. Scribes sometimes altered the text of a Gospel in order to make it agree with a parallel account in another Gospel. In some cases additions or alterations were made in order to give doctrinal emphasis, but these are very few in the New Testament books.

The task of the textual critic is, taking into consideration all these processes, to seek to discover the true text —the words which were actually written by the author.

For this purpose, he has to examine the evidence of MSS. of various types, before the introduction of printing put an end to the period of written copies. (The first edition of the printed Greek New Testament to be published was that of Erasmus in 1516.) In the case of the New Testament the material which is at our disposal for ascertaining the true text is vast. We have many more ancient copies of the Gospels than we have, for instance, of the works of contemporary writers like Horace and Tacitus or the Greek philosopher Epictetus. We can confidently say that we are more sure of the actual words of the writers of the New Testament books than we are of the true text of any other ancient authors.

THE MATERIALS OF TEXTUAL CRITICISM

In the case of the New Testament, these fall into three classes:

(a) *Greek MSS.* The earliest ones were written on papyrus. This was made from the pith of the stem of the papyrus plant, which grew by the Nile and other places. A layer of strips was placed over another layer, at right angles, and these were glued and pressed together to form a sheet of writing material. A piece of this about the size of a foolscap or quarto sheet of paper could be purchased in the market-place of a town in the Roman world and papyrus sheets were used for private and business correspondence, for bills and receipts and contracts. Specimens of such have been dug up from the rubbish heaps of Egyptian villages, where they have been preserved under the dry sand for over a thousand years. A book, or more strictly a roll, was formed by sticking together a number of papyrus sheets to form a long piece which was rolled up around a wooden stick. Sometimes a number of sheets were put together to form a book with pages—called a codex— and there is evidence that this process was particularly favoured by the Christians.

The earliest MSS. we possess of New Testament books are on papyrus. Many of them are mere fragments; the oldest is a small piece of the Fourth Gospel, which was discovered in a collection at the John Rylands Library in Manchester in 1935. It was written probably about A.D. 150. In 1934 the British Museum acquired some scraps of papyrus which were found to be fragments of a hitherto unknown Gospel, dating from the middle of the second century. In 1931 Mr. A. Chester Beatty, an American collector, acquired in Egypt a large number of papyrus sheets containing the Gospels and Paul's letters, as well as other books of the Bible.

Papyrus came to be superseded as a writing material, at least for books, by vellum. This had been employed since the first century B.C. but it did not come into general use among the Christians until the beginning of the fourth century A.D. It was prepared from the skins of animals and was not used in the form of a roll; a number of sheets were folded together to form a quire, and the quires were bound together as in a modern book. Vellum was more expensive than papyrus but was durable. MSS. in vellum, running into hundreds of pages, have been preserved in a remarkably fine condition. One advantage to the Christians was that it was no longer necessary to have four separate rolls if one wanted a copy of the Gospels; they could all be included within the covers of one book.

Some of the finest vellum MSS. of the New Testament date from the fourth and fifth centuries—the Vatican Codex (known by the symbol B), in the Vatican library at Rome, the Codex Bezae (known as D), at Cambridge, the Codex Alexandrinus (known as A), in the British Museum, and the Sinai Codex (known by the letter ℵ—Aleph, the first letter of the Hebrew alphabet). This was discovered in the monastery of St. Catherine on Mount Sinai by the German scholar Tischendorf in 1843 and it was in Russia until 1934, when the British government and people purchased it for £100,000 and it was placed in the British Museum. These are all uncial MSS.—written in old Greek capital letters—and they constitute four great Bibles, for they contain the whole or portions of the Old Testament in Greek as well as New Testament books. There are other uncials, the discovery of some of which is fairly recent, such as the Freer MS. of the Gospels, in Washington, and the Koridethi Codex, discovered in the Caucasus mountains. A second class of MSS. is known as minuscules and these are written in the smaller running hand which superseded the use of the old capital letters. There are over 2,300 minuscule MSS. of the New Testament or portions of it.

(b) *Translations*. The books of the New Testament, written in Greek, had to be translated if they were to be made available to people living on the fringe of the Roman Empire. The Christian churches in the Empire were missionary centres; we see in the Acts of the Apostles how Antioch became a missionary base for work in Syria and Asia Minor. Rome similarly became the headquarters for work in Italy and North Africa, and Alexandria the centre for Egyptian expansion. At

Antioch the Christian writings were translated into
Syriac, at Rome they were put into Latin, at Alexandria into the Egyptian dialects and at Caesarea into
Armenian. Later on there came 'secondary versions'
—translations of these translations—such as the
Georgian (made from the Armenian), the Arabic
(from Syriac and Coptic) and the first English versions
(from the Latin).

The most important of these is the Latin version.
The oldest Latin translations probably were made in
the second century; this became the standard Bible of
the church at Rome until Jerome revised the existing
MSS. and produced the Vulgate in 382. As with the
Greek books, so with the versions we have not the
first MSS. but copies. Some of these are of late date,
but they are valuable since they frequently bear witness
to a text (the Greek underlying the translation) which
is earlier than that in our oldest vellum Greek MSS.
Here also of course there is the possibility of slips and
alterations by scribes.

(c) *Quotations in Christian Writers.* The leaders of the
Church frequently referred to the Gospels or the
Epistles in their writings and quoted from or commented
on them and other books of the Bible. From their
references we can learn what text of the New Testament
they were accustomed to use. This evidence has to be
used with caution, for they themselves would sometimes make slips in copying or would quote from
memory without troubling to refer to a roll or codex.
Their works, too, in turn were copied by scribes, who
might alter a quotation to agree with a reading with
which they were more familiar. The chief value of the
early quotations is that, if we know where the writer
was living at the time, they help us to fix the locality

Having discovered what he wrote, we next have to find out his meaning or discover the source of his information or its significance. This may not at first be at all plain and further thought may be necessary. This is not, of course, a perfect parallel, but it is sufficiently close to say that when we sought to find out what our correspondent wrote we were practising Lower or Textual Criticism and when we tried to understand it we were practising Higher Criticism.

This book deals mainly with matters of Higher Criticism—questions of the composition of the Gospels, their dates and authorship. Matters of Textual Criticism will only occasionally occur.

THE GROWTH OF THE NEW TESTAMENT

In many ways it is a great advantage to have four Gospels in the New Testament instead of only one. We are able to see the story of Jesus through the eyes of four different men, each of whom wrote for a distinctive type of reader. There is evidence that in the early centuries there were other Gospels, which were rejected and have now in most cases almost completely disappeared. The Unknown Gospel fragment discovered in 1934 was probably compiled from our Gospels; but even in the small scrap of papyrus which contains the story of the leper who came to Jesus (Mark 1: 40–45), there is the additional statement that the leper caught his disease through 'journeying with lepers and eating with them in the inn'. We know from quotations and references in Christian writers that there was a Gospel according to the Hebrews, a Gospel according to the Egyptians and Gospels attributed to Philip, Thomas and Peter. But if we compare the contents of these, as far as we know them, with our Gospels, we see their inferiority.

Our Gospels are called the canonical ones. The word 'canon' comes from a Semitic and then a Greek word which originally meant a rule. It constituted a standard—for measurement and then for judgment and conduct. Since a rule had on it a number of marks, the word came also to mean a list. Each church had at first its own canon and churches often disagreed regarding the authorship of certain books and their place on the authoritative list. Some churches accepted the Epistle to the Hebrews while others did not and there was hesitancy in some places about the Book of Revelation and some of the smaller non-Pauline epistles. Other churches included books which are now outside the New Testament, such as the Shepherd of Hermas and the Epistle of Barnabas, both of which are actually bound up with the New Testament in the Codex Sinaiticus.

Eventually the authority of the churches of Rome and Carthage prevailed and their collection of twenty-seven Christian writings was urged by Jerome and Augustine of Hippo and became the New Testament which we have today. The main streams of Christianity today all have the same New Testament— Eastern (Orthodox), Roman (Catholic) and non-Roman (Protestant, both episcopal and non-episcopal). There are, however, still some ancient churches which have not quite the same number of books. The Syrian church of South India has not the Book of Revelation and four minor Catholic epistles, while the Ethiopian church has eight additional books.

THE NEW TESTAMENT IN ENGLAND

English people, unless they learn Hellenistic Greek, in which the New Testament books were written (a task not of insuperable difficulty to anyone who has shown any ability at all to learn a foreign language, and much easier than many languages, ancient and modern), must content themselves with a translation. The first Bibles brought to this country were no doubt Latin ones, carried by Roman Christians, and the first English versions were made from the Latin. Alfred the Great had portions of the Bible translated into Anglo-Saxon and the Venerable Bede had already translated the Gospels, finishing, according to the well-known story, the last words of the Fourth Gospel with his dying breath (735). The first complete English version of the New Testament was that of John Wyclif (1382); it was a translation of the Latin Vulgate. William Tyndale was the first to have printed an English version of the Bible (1528) and he was able to use not only the Latin translation but also the Greek text published by Erasmus in 1516. Subsequently English versions multipled—Coverdale's, the Great Bible, the Bishops' Bible, to name only a few—until by the beginning of the seventeenth century there were at least sixteen different translations of the Bible in English. King James I called for the publication of yet another translation, which was produced as the King's Bible in 1611 and became known as the Authorized Version. This version was eventually recognized as superior to its predecessors and held the field for nearly three hundred years.

Towards the end of the nineteenth century it was realized by scholars and the leaders of the churches

that many discoveries had been made which necessit-
ated at least a revision of the Authorized Version. The
translators in 1611 had used MSS. of comparatively
late date, which naturally contained corruptions and
scribal errors. They could not compare this material
with more reliable MSS., for of the four great Bibles
mentioned above, the Codex Bezae was the only one
available to them. They could not consult the Vatican
Codex, in the Pope's library at Rome, and the Sinai
Codex had not been discovered. Much additional
textual material had thus accumulated since 1611.
In addition extensive research had been made in the
course of 260 years into the Greek language of the
early Christian centuries and much valuable material
had come to light to illustrate words and phrases and
conceptions used by the New Testament writers. For
fourteen years the best scholars of the country worked
at their task and at length the Revised Version of the
New Testament was issued in 1881 and that of the
whole Bible in 1884.

For purity of text, accuracy and fidelity to the
original writings, the Revised Version is incomparably
superior to any previous English version. In more
recent times, further translations have been produced,
some by individuals such as Dr. Weymouth, Dr. Moffatt
and Dr. E. V. Rieu, some anonymously, such as the
Twentieth Century New Testament, and some by com-
mittees of scholars representing all branches of the
Church, such as the Revised Standard Version, which
is in use in the United States of America and Canada.
At the time of writing a commission is busily engaged
on producing a new version of the Bible in English,
which will be textually accurate and also presentable
as literature.

The New Testament as we have it is thus the result of a long process—the collection of material by the different writers, copying MSS. by diligent scribes, translation for missionary purposes, interpretation and study by scholars. If we have some knowledge of this process and of the many men and women, of all languages, races and ages, who have contributed to this, it will help us to appreciate and understand not only their great labours but also the message of the New Testament itself.

CHAPTER II

THE ORAL PERIOD

The Gospel before the Gospels

The word 'gospel' is generally used to indicate a book, of which there are four in the New Testament. Originally, however, it meant not a book but a proclamation. The English word comes from two Anglo-Saxon words, *God* and *spell*, meaning 'God-narrative' (or possibly 'good story'). It is an English translation of the Greek word *euaggelion*, which, through the Latin *evangelium*, has come into our language in words such as 'evangelist' and 'evangelical'.

The Christian gospel was thus originally a message which was spoken, not written down. Using the related verb, Luke characterises the announcement of the birth of Jesus as bringing 'good tidings of great joy' (Luke 2: 10). Paul uses the term in speaking of his own message —'the gospel which I preach' (Gal. 2: 2). He calls this 'my gospel' (Rom. 2: 16; 16: 25) and refers to the gospel which was proclaimed by those also who were associated with him in the Christian mission (1 Thess. 1: 5; 2 Cor. 4: 3). The word is used in this sense in Mark 1: 14–15, where the writer says that Jesus 'came into Galilee, preaching the gospel of God', that the Kingdom of God was at hand. The 'heading' to this book combines both these senses—the good news preached by Jesus and the good news about Jesus—'the beginning of the gospel of Jesus Christ' (Mark 1: 1).

We can see from a study of the speeches which are recorded in the Acts of the Apostles, and also from Paul's letters, what the early Christian gospel was. It centred in the proclamation of the coming of Jesus. History, the preachers declared, led up to that (and since history to them meant the story of the Hebrews, they naturally turned to the Old Testament for confirmation and illustration); a new era of history began with him (this meant for them that the Messianic age was a present reality); and the era would be closed with his triumph (which they sometimes pictured in terms borrowed from Jewish apocalyptic). The proclamation therefore would inevitably include some account of the coming of Jesus, his life, his teaching, his death and resurrection. It may seem at first that there is little reference to this in Paul's letters, but this is because he is not giving his teaching to his converts for the first time. He is advising them on practical or theological problems, which they themselves have often raised, and reminding them of the things which they should have already known. In the speeches in the Acts, by Peter, Paul and others, brief reference is made to the life and work of Jesus, especially when those who were being addressed had not had the opportunity of seeing him for themselves or were possibly hearing about him for the first time, as at Caesarea when Peter addressed Cornelius and his household (Acts 10:36–43). The speeches in the Acts are only summaries of what was said and Peter's address was no doubt much longer than this and probably included some detailed information about the life of Jesus.

But the story of Jesus, as part of the proclamation of the good news and as a necessary part of the instruction of would-be members of the Church, was not written down at once. It was passed on by word of mouth. There are three main reasons why the narrative was not immediately committed to writing in a more permanent form:

(i) The early Christians were not literary people or folk with a great amount of leisure. Paul reminded his converts that their ranks included 'not many wise after the flesh, not many mighty, not many noble' (1 Cor. 1: 26)—as this world viewed them—and most of the Christians of the first century would not have the ability or the time to set out a written account. Writing a book was a long and expensive business, as it had to be set down by hand on sheets of papyrus or a roll. Very few people could afford to possess books of their own. The members of a typical Jewish household in the time of Jesus, for instance, would not have a Bible of their own. If they wished to refer to a passage from the Old Testament, they would have to go to the synagogue and consult the Rabbi. The early Christians, most of them busy working people and many of them slaves, were not people accustomed to handling or writing books.

(ii) The Christians were too busy proclaiming their message and living it, to bother about its permanent preservation. The urgent matter for them was for everyone to hear the gospel. This was the more important in view of their expectation that the 'end of the age' would soon come. They thought that Christ himself would reappear in glory and would bring the resurrection and judgment of men, ushering in a new age in which the Kingdom of God would have fully come. Paul himself thought, at one time in his life at any rate, that his own generation would be the last—'we that are alive, that are left for the coming of the

Lord . . .' (1 Thess. 4: 15). Men must be told the
message at once, before it was too late. As this 'consummation of the age' was so near, there would be no
point in writing down accounts for the benefit of future
generations.

(iii) The story would be remembered, without being
written down. The people in the ancient world had
extraordinary powers of memory. This is still the case
in the east and in other places where people do not
rely on the written word as we do. Among the Jews,
the Rabbis used to instruct their pupils orally; their
teaching was learned by heart, without any written
notes. Jesus himself probably adopted this method, in
instructing his own disciples. They in turn would pass
on his teaching and would tell of incidents at which
they themselves had been present; their hearers would
remember them and be able to relate them to others.
In the Christian meetings, the stories of Jesus and his
teaching would be repeated, to encourage church-
members. They would also be included in the instruction given to converts. Missionaries would relate them
in their preaching.

FORM CRITICISM

This 'oral period', before the completion of a written
Gospel, lasted about a generation. During this time
the tradition was necessarily fragmentary. Nobody
would remember the whole of the story, as one connected account such as appears in our Gospels, and it
would not be related as a whole. Separate incidents
and passages of Jesus' teaching would be remembered
by different individuals. As these were repeated, there
would be a tendency for the stories to assume something

like a set form or pattern; they would also tend to fall into different types. We can still see traces of this as we read our written Gospels, for the stories found there can be classified; some of them have their chief interest in a statement by Jesus, others are stories of healing or other wonders, some of them are about the companions of Jesus.

Much study has been given to this subject during the past thirty years and scholars have been examining and classifying the oral 'forms' which are still discernible in the written accounts. This study is called Form Criticism (or Form History; German *Formgeschichte*, for the Germans were the pioneers in this branch of New Testament criticism). According to the Form Critics, we are able to place the material found in our Gospels into roughly four categories, corresponding to four types of oral material which were in circulation in the first generation of the early Church.

(i) Pronouncement-Stories (Vincent Taylor's term), or Paradigms (models—Martin Dibelius' term). These are stories which are linked with some saying of Jesus, with which the account concludes. Many of the short narratives in the Gospels seem to have their climax in a statement of Jesus. The following are typical examples: Mark 2: 16–17 (Jesus and outcasts); 2: 23–27 (the treatment of the Sabbath); 3: 31–35 (Jesus' true relations); 9: 38–40 (the exorcist); 10: 13–15 (the reception of children); 10: 17–21 (the rich man); 12: 13–17 (the question of tribute); Luke 12: 13–15 (the question of the inheritance); 17: 20–21 (the coming of the Kingdom).

In these instances Jesus spoke on topics which were not only of interest to his immediate hearers but also of importance to the early Christians—the relation of

Christianity to Judaism and Jewish institutions like the Sabbath and to the Roman rule, the right attitude towards 'outsiders' and children and rich people. When differences arose or there was discussion in the church about such matters, a story about Jesus which threw light upon the matter would be recalled and the narrative was remembered primarily for the sake of the saying to which it led up.

(ii) Miracle-stories. These tell of the power of Jesus in healing people and performing mighty works. Typical instances are Mark 1 : 40–45 (the leper); 5 : 1–20 (the madman of the Gerasene country); 5: 21–43 (Jairus' daughter); 9: 14–29 (the epileptic son); Luke 7: 11–17 (the widow's son). These stories generally follow much the same 'pattern'. There is given first a statement of the disease; then follows an appeal by the sufferer to Jesus. He makes his response—perhaps a question or a command; then comes the cure. Afterwards there is generally a comment—exclamations of wonder from the crowd or criticism from Jesus' opponents. Such stories would be of value not only in the Christian assemblies but also for missionary preaching. Heathen people, familiar with stories of miracles worked by the gods or their devotees, would be interested in these and would perhaps be able to appreciate the difference between these simply-told narratives and the marvellous and sometimes fantastic tales of pagan religions.

(iii) Biographical sketches of Jesus or of people who were associated with him. (Vincent Taylor calls these Stories about Jesus, while Dibelius' term is Tales.) Here there is more of a literary interest and it is not surprising to find many of them in Luke's Gospel. Accounts of the activities of Jesus include the visit to

Nazareth (Mark 6: 1–6), a story about his childhood
(Luke 2: 41–51), his baptism (Mark 1: 9–11) and
temptations (Luke 4: 1–13; Matt. 4: 1–11), the incident at Caesarea Philippi (Mark 8: 27ff) and the
transfiguration (Mark 9: 2ff).

Sketches of other people in this category include the
story of the sinful woman (Luke 7: 36–50), Mary and
Martha (Luke 10: 38–42), Zacchaeus (Luke 19: 1–10)
and the call of the first disciples (Mark 1: 16–20; cf.
Luke 5: 1–11). In these cases there is given a fuller
description of the circumstances than is found in the
Pronouncement-stories, and the emphasis is not so
much on the saying of Jesus or on his healing power as
on the characters of the people concerned. The early
Christians would in this way have knowledge of the
people in Jesus' own circle and his dealings with various
types.

We must, however, beware of thinking that these
three types of narrative form hard and fast categories
(and we must certainly not imagine that the early
Christians deliberately conceived these 'forms' and
carefully arranged the oral material to fit into them!).
The types sometimes overlap. It is, for instance,
difficult to say definitely whether the story about
Jesus' boyhood (Luke 2: 41–51) is best regarded as a
Biography-story or a Pronouncement-story, since it concludes with a statement by Jesus himself. The narrative
about Zacchaeus similarly might be put in either of
these categories. The account of the cure of Bartimaeus
(Mark 10: 46–52) might be classed as a Biography-
story, since the man is named, or as a Miracle-Story.
The cure of the centurion's servant (Luke 7: 2–10;
Matt. 8: 5–13) is a Miracle-story but it is also a
Pronouncement-story, having its climax in a word of

Jesus about the faith of a Gentile. We use the categories to help us to classify the material and to see more clearly the interests of the early Christians and their motives in preserving the oral traditions.

(iv) The teaching of Jesus, in sayings and parables. Just as the sayings of the Rabbis were remembered and treasured by their disciples, so the words of Jesus were repeated by the first apostles and passed on by word of mouth. Many of the statements of Jesus in the Gospels have no definite time or place associated with their utterance and they were probably repeated in the early Church as detached utterances (e.g. Luke 12: 22ff; 17: 20–21). In some instances two writers do not agree about the place or time of an utterance of Jesus. Thus the saying about the world-wide nature of the Kingdom of God is attached in Matthew to the story of the centurion's servant (Matt. 8: 11–12), while Luke places it in another situation, on the way to Jerusalem (Luke 13: 28–29). The parables of the mustard seed and the leaven are placed in Matthew in the midst of a whole chapter devoted to parables (Matt. 13: 31–33) but they are isolated, in another situation, in Luke (13: 18–21). This supports the view that, like the stories, the sayings and parables of Jesus were told in the early Church in a somewhat fragmentary form; it would be left to the compiler of a written account later to set them out in order and to link them together.

THE WRITING OF THE GOSPELS

All this material was thus in circulation in the early Church before the writing of the first of our Gospels. The episodes were told and retold as occasion demanded; the sayings and parables were recited. But we must not make too sharp a distinction between the oral and the writing period. We must not suppose that at a particular moment the disciples suddenly ceased to relate the stories and depended thenceforth simply on a written account. The two periods necessarily overlapped. Probably within twenty years of the crucifixion a collection of Jesus' sayings was made and written down. It is possible that some of the incidents also were written down, for use by preachers and teachers. This material was, however, still fragmentary in character. No attempt was made at a connected written account of Jesus' work from its beginning, after his baptism by John, to the end, culminating in the crucifixion and resurrection. And the oral material still continued to be told.

This material—mostly oral with probably some in writing—was the matter out of which the first of our written Gospels was made. The writer was not an author or biographer, in the modern sense. He was rather an editor or compiler, making use of the material already to a large extent familiar to his readers. In order to form a connected narrative, he had to link together the separate episodes and sayings. He introduced them with notes of time and place and supplied phrases to connect an incident with the preceding paragraph. Sometimes he added comments or gave a summary of Jesus' work and teaching (e.g. Mark 6: 55–56; cf. Matt. 4: 23–25). Explanatory notes were added, to help readers unfamiliar with the situation in Palestine (e.g. Mark 7: 3–4). Occasionally comments were added for the edification of the readers.

An illustration of this process of collecting and editing is provided by the accounts in Mark 2 and 3: 1–6.

The writer (either Mark himself or a predecessor whose work he used at this point) gathered together a Miracle story—the paralysed man—(2: 1–12), the call of Levi, a disciple (2: 14), a dispute over a meal with tax-collectors (2: 15–17), a discussion about fasting (2: 18–22), an incident on the Sabbath (2: 23–27)—a Pronouncement-story—and the cure of a man's withered hand on the Sabbath (3: 1–6). He thus produced a series of 'conflict-stories', in which the opposition to Jesus reaches a climax in a plot against him (3: 6). In Mark 9: 39–50 we have a collection of sayings which have little connection with each other, except that they are linked together by the repetition of certain 'key-words' and ideas. In Luke 16 a parable about a dishonest steward (vv. 1–8) is followed by a series of sayings about wealth and its responsibilities (vv. 9–13) which have no connection with the parable and very little relation with each other. In a similar way the writer of Matthew made a collection of parables about the Kingdom of God (13: 1–50), while Luke put together three parables about the lost in chapter 15.

There were a number of reasons why the oral period eventually came to an end and why the good news was committed to writing:

(a) The original disciples were going. James, the son of Zebedee, was the first of the twelve to be put to death (Acts 12: 2); this occurred about A.D. 42. By the second half of the first century it is possible that others had suffered a similar fate; in any case the apostles would be scattered in different parts of the world and were not immediately available with their first-hand reminiscences of the life of Jesus. The question inevitably arose: What was to happen when they were all gone? Would the oral story be lost or so changed by unauthorised additions that it could not longer be relied on?

(b) The first persecution of the Church by the Romans accentuated this impulse to write. In A.D. 64, after the great fire of Rome, the emperor Nero was led to blame the Christians for it and attempted to stamp out the Church. It is probable that Peter and Paul were both put to death at this time. The Christians, deprived of their leaders and meeting together secretly, would want the story in a more permanent form than the oral traditions. Those who were suffering in this way would want to be assured of the historical origins of their faith, and others, drawn to the Church by the steadfastness of the Christians under persecution, would require something more than mere stories handed on by word of mouth.

(c) In A.D. 70 the Romans, after taking five years to crush the revolt of the Jews, took Jerusalem and destroyed the city and Temple. Before the final assault the Jewish Christians had fled across the Jordan to Pella. Jewish Christianity ceased practically to be of any importance in the Roman Empire, and the Church became almost an exclusively Gentile movement. This meant that Christianity was now cut off from its roots. The end of Jerusalem meant that the scene of the last days of Jesus' life was wiped out. The story must be preserved in a permanent and tangible form if it was not to become a tradition comparable to the legends of Greek and Roman 'sons of the gods', with no definite historical and geographical location.

(d) The needs of Christian worship were probably another factor. The early Church followed the form of worship in the synagogue, in having a reading from the

Old Testament. Churches which had received letters
from Paul, or possessed copies of those letters, probably supplemented the Old Testament reading by
extracts from these. Possibly some of the teaching of
Jesus, already in written form, was also read at times.
But there would be a demand, as time went on, for a
fuller account of Jesus' ministry, which could be read
consecutively, week after week.

So the telling of the stories gradually ceased and men
came to rely on the written accounts. So now we turn
to consider the Gospels as we have them in the New
Testament.

CHAPTER III

THE SYNOPTIC PROBLEM

Ever since the second century it has been customary
to draw a distinction between the first three Gospels
and the Fourth. We shall later see specific ways in
which the Fourth Gospel is distinctive; it will be
sufficient at the moment to say that it differs in chronology, in the presentation of the events narrated, in the
style and the matter of Jesus' teaching and in the place
of most of his public work. In contrast to this, the first
three Gospels stand together; they give a similar outline of the work and ministry of Jesus, seen from the
same point of view to a large extent. Because of this
they are classed together as the Synoptic Gospels (from
two Greek words, *sun*—together—and *opsis*—a view or
sight). The term also relates to the fact that many
passages in the three books can be put in parallel
columns and thus 'seen together' in a Synopsis.

A problem exists whenever there are facts which
have to be accounted for. The scientist, faced with a
series of phenomena, proposes a theory or hypothesis
to account for them. He tests the hypothesis. If he
finds that it works and most satisfactorily explains the
phenomena, the hypothesis becomes the accepted solution of the problem. The Synoptic Problem arises from
the facts about the contents of the three Gospels—facts
which are plain to any careful reader. These facts are
enumerated below, so that it may be appreciated
what the problem actually is. Then three questions

have to be answered: Why is it that the three books are so much alike? At the same time, why do they differ in many ways? What is the solution of the problem which most fully accounts for the phenomena?

THE PROBLEM

(i) The similarities between the three Gospels. These are of two kinds. First, all three books have the same general outline of the life of Jesus. There are four main divisions of his public work:

(a) His ministry in Galilee (Mark 1 to 7: 23; Matt. 3 to 15: 20; Luke 3 to 9: 17). This section tells the story of John the Baptist and his preaching, the baptism of Jesus and his temptations, his healing ministry; his teaching in synagogues and the open air, the opposition to him from the religious leaders and his choosing and commission of twelve disciples.

(b) Journeys in the north, outside Galilee (Mark 7: 24 to 9: 50; Matt. 15: 21 to 18: 35; Luke 9: 18–50). Here Jesus goes to Phoenicia, to Bethsaida and to Caesarea Philippi (in the territory of Herod Philip), where he is acknowledged as Messiah. The transfiguration and teaching follow.

(c) The journey to Jerusalem (Mark 10; Matt. 19–20; Luke 9: 51 to 19: 28). Jesus leaves Galilee and proceeds south, eventually arriving at Jericho on the road to Jerusalem.

(d) The last day in Jerusalem (Mark 11–16; Matt. 21–28; Luke 19: 29 to 24: 53). This section includes the entry into the city, the events of 'Holy week', teaching of Jesus, the trial, crucifixion and resurrection appearances.

One would naturally expect the writer of a Gospel to include much of this matter but the remarkable thing is that all three include it mainly in the same order. When they do occasionally diverge, they always return to the common order.

There is hence considerable overlapping and this raises a second aspect. When we study parallel passages, either of incident or of teaching, we find a remarkable verbal similarity; sometimes the wording is almost identical for whole sentences. The following passages are typical:

The healing of the paralytic (Matt. 9: 1–8; Mark 2: 1–12; Luke 5: 17–26).

The question of fasting (Matt. 9: 14–17; Mark 2: 18–22; Luke 5: 33–39).

The parable of the mustard seed (Matt. 13: 31–32; Mark 4: 30–32; Luke 13: 18–19).

The feeding of the five thousand (Matt. 14: 13–21; Mark 6: 30–44; Luke 9: 10–17).

The rich man (Matt. 19: 16–22; Mark 10: 17–22; Luke 18: 18–23).

The healing of Bartimaeus (Matt. 20: 29–34; Mark 10: 46–52; Luke 18: 35–43).

The challenge to Jesus' authority (Matt. 21: 23–27; Mark 11: 27–33; Luke 20: 1–8).

The question of tribute (Matt. 22: 15–22; Mark 12: 13–17; Luke 20: 20–26).

Peter's denials (Matt. 26: 69–75; Mark 14: 66–72; Luke 22: 56–62).

In other cases the parallel matter is found in only two Gospels. Occasionally this is in Mark and either Matthew or Luke but most frequently it is in Matthew and Luke only. The following are typical passages:

The calling of disciples (Matt. 4: 18–22; Mark 1: 16–20).

Jesus and scribal tradition (Matt. 15: 1–20; Mark 7: 1–23).

The sons of Zebedee (Matt. 20: 20–28; Mark 10: 35–45).

The anointing at Bethany (Matt. 26: 6–13; Mark 14: 3–9).

The widow's mites (Mark 12: 41–44; Luke 21: 1–4).

John the Baptist's preaching (Matt. 3: 7–10; Luke 3: 7–9).

Teaching on judging others (Matt. 7: 1–5; Luke 6: 37–38, 41–42).

Teaching on anxiety (Matt. 6: 25–33; Luke 12: 22–31).

The healing of a centurion's servant (Matt. 8: 5–13; Luke 7: 1–10).

John's question from prison (Matt. 11: 2–19; Luke 7: 18–35).

The parable of the leaven (Matt. 13: 33; Luke 13: 20–21).

Jesus' lament over Jerusalem (Matt. 23: 37–39; Luke 13: 34–35).

Anyone who studies these parallel passages carefully must be convinced that a problem exists and that there must be some connection between the three Gospels.

(ii) The differences between the three Gospels. The Synoptics are not entirely alike. If they were, there would be no real problem; they would obviously be copies of each other or of an earlier work. There are again two ways in which the differences appear—in the order of events and in the wording in parallel passages.

There are variations within the same general Synoptic scheme of events. The cures of the demoniac, the woman and Jairus' daughter are all told in this order in the three Gospels, but in Mark and Luke they come after Jesus' teaching in parables, but before it in Matthew. The account of the rejection of Jesus at Nazareth comes at much the same point in Matthew (13: 53–58) and in Mark (6: 1–6), but is considerably earlier in Luke (4: 16–30). Teaching which is given in Mark (13: 9–13) in Jerusalem in the last week is said in Matthew (10: 17–22) to have been delivered in Galilee, early in the ministry.

In parallel passages the wording is generally not exactly the same. Study of the passages enumerated above will have amply demonstrated this. Sometimes it seems as if one Gospel and sometimes another has the more vivid phrase or graphic description or has reproduced more faithfully the note of Jesus' teaching.

A further difference is that each of the Gospels has matter which is not found elsewhere. This is very small in the case of Mark—only about thirty verses, consisting of one parable, two healing acts and a few particulars here and there in the narrative. Matthew's has a considerable amount of Jesus' teaching which is not in Mark or Luke and some additional particulars in common narratives. Luke has a large amount of matter peculiar to this book consisting of both, incidents and parables and sayings. Both Matthew and Luke record stories about the birth and infancy of Jesus, but the accounts are quite different. At the end of each of these two Gospels there are recorded appearances of Jesus after the resurrection, but again they differ and even conflict in some particulars.

Just as the similarities show that there must be some connection between the three Gospels, so the differences show that they must have been written independently. This is confirmed by a reading of the books; each writer tells the story from his own point of view. The opening words of each Gospel well illustrate this. Matthew starts with a genealogy of Jesus, like a typical Jewish book, similar to some of the Old Testament books. Mark has a 'heading', which sounds like a proclamation, and then, after a passing reference to the Old Testament, plunges into the story of John the Baptist—blunt and straight-forward, like the remainder of the book. Luke commences with a carefully worded introduction and dedication to Theophilus, and his is indeed the most literary of all the Gospels.

These facts constitute the Synoptic Problem. However 'uncritical' a reader may claim to be, he cannot fail to be struck by these facts and if he desires to understand the Gospels fully he is bound to proceed to the questions: What is the relation between the three books? Why are they so much alike and yet so different? What can we deduce from this study about the writers and about the methods which they used in composing their books?

SOLUTIONS OF THE SYNOPTIC PROBLEM

To these questions various answers have been given:

(i) One traditional answer has been that God inspired the evangelists to write and so they must agree when they record the teaching and acts of Jesus. There are two main difficulties in this view. One is that it conceives God as dictating to men what they were to put down, without allowing for their natural human inclination and ability. This is at variance with all that we know of the ways of God with men and with all that the Bible teaches about inspiration. The second objection is that the theory does not fit the facts. While it might be held to account for the similarities and verbal parallels, it does not account for the differences. Why should God inspire one man to say that James and John came to Jesus with a request (Mark 10: 35) but tell another man to write that their mother came? (Matt. 20: 20). Why should he dictate, 'How canst thou say . . .?' to one writer (Luke 6: 42), but 'How wilt thou say . . .?' to another? (Matt. 7: 4). Why should he instruct Mark to write a full and vivid account of many a healing act of Jesus (e.g. 5: 1–20 and 9: 14–29) but inspire Matthew to write a shorter and considerably less vivid account? (8: 28–34 and 17: 14–20). Why should Matthew's Gospel say that the Roman centurion came himself to Jesus with a request that he would heal his Servant (8: 5ff), while in Luke's account the Centurion never appears at all but sends his message through others (7: 3ff), if both writers were verbally inspired by God?

If it is replied that God must work through the interests of each individual and leave an author to write in his own style and use his own intelligence and critical capacity, this surrenders the whole case for 'verbal inspiration'. This is the very problem with which we are concerned—why three accounts should differ, as well as why they agree—and it is no real answer to say simply that they were 'inspired' to do so.

This theory does not arise from a study of the books themselves and the problem which they present but from a preconceived notion of 'inspiration' which will not bear examination when confronted with the facts.

(ii) Another traditional explanation is the 'oral hypothesis'. Each writer is held to be dependent on the oral tradition, such as we have discussed in chapter II. They wrote independently but happened to use similar words and phrases and kept to the same general order because they faithfully adhered to the oral accounts.

The first difficulty here is that this theory regards the oral traditions as having assumed a fixed form not only in the relation of particular incidents or sections of teaching but also in the general order of the narrative. There is no ground for this assumption and it is very unlikely in itself; the traditions circulated in the Church as separate episodes, not as one connected historical narrative, and we can still discern the fragmentary nature of the stories even in our written Gospels. It is also very improbable that the oral traditions would have attained such fixity of form and wording and that three writers, rendering the tradition independently and probably in different parts of the Roman world, would agree in their phraseology and order of events in the way that the three Synoptists do.

This theory further does not explain the variations either in wording or in order. In some instances the verbal differences are due to stylistic and grammatical alterations. This suggests not oral traditions only but a written document which is being used. How also are we to account, on this view, for the matter found in Matthew and Luke but not in Mark—again often similar in wording but with subtle and characteristic alterations—or the matter which is peculiar to Matthew or to Luke? If this was part of the 'standard' oral tradition, why was it omitted by the other writers?

We are therefore forced to the conclusion that something more than simply oral tradition lies behind the three accounts and that there is a literary connection between them. A documentary hypothesis must be examined. The possibilities here are many—that all three used the same document or more than one document or that one Gospel was written first and the other two made use of it—if so, which one?

(iii) The first documentary theory was that Matthew was written first and that Mark abbreviated this book. Augustine (about A.D. 400) suggested this; he regarded Mark as the 'attendant and abbreviator of Matthew' (*pedisequus et breviator Matthaei*). This view was put forward because Mark's Gospel is shorter than Matthew's and much of the Matthaean matter is not found in Mark.

There are two main objections here. The first impression of Mark, as being shorter than Matthew, is deceptive, for in parallel narratives Mark is almost always the longer account. The following narratives as told in the two books occupy the number of verses indicated:

The healing of the paralytic: Mark 12, Matthew 7 verses.

The Gerasene madman: Mark 20, Matthew 7 verses.

Jairus' daughter and the healing of a woman: Mark 23, Matthew 9 verses.

The feeding of the five thousand: Mark 15, Matthew 9 verses.

The healing of the epileptic son: Mark 16, Matthew 7 verses.

In these and other instances Mark's narrative is much more vivid and lifelike than Matthew's, which is often tame in comparison and omits vital points. No 'abbreviator' of Matthew would take these narratives and make them into Mark's fuller accounts. The reverse is much more likely.

The other objection is that so much valuable matter found in Matthew is missing in Mark. Why should an 'abbreviator' or editor omit the Sermon on the Mount and parables such as the treasure and the pearl merchant, the labourers in the vineyard, the ten virgins, the sheep and the goats? Why should he ignore the story of Jesus' birth and infancy and commence his account with John the Baptist's work, in the abrupt way that Mark does?

(iv) A documentary theory popular in some circles in the last century was the view that there was a primitive written gospel which was used by all three writers. (German critics called this *Urevangelium*.) This might account for the places where the three agree in order of events or in wording. But it does not take into account the matter which is common to Luke and Matthew, but not found in Mark. If this was in the primitive Gospel, why did Mark omit it? Neither can it account for the matter peculiar to Matthew or to Luke. One must assume here also, as with the hypothesis of the priority of Matthew, that the writer of Mark deliberately omitted much that was valuable of the teaching and activities of Jesus and yet managed to produce a book which gives a straightforward impression of a simple and vivid narrative.

It is thus difficult to assign a limit to this supposed primitive Gospel. If we limit its contents to the parallels in all three Gospels, we are making it practically identical with our Mark; this is quite a feasible suggestion, but in the process the primitive document, as a separate identity, has disappeared! There is also the great difficulty that no trace of such a document can be found and there is no support in early Church writings for its existence.

This view, like that of Augustine, has now generally been abandoned and we are driven back to seeking the connection in the Gospels as we have them now. In the next two paragraphs we shall have to anticipate the discussion in the three following chapters, but it is convenient to insert here in summary form the conclusions which may be regarded as established to the satisfaction of the vast majority of New Testament scholars today.

(v) The two-source theory holds that Mark was the first Gospel to be written and was used as a source by the authors of Matthew and Luke. This was first suggested by Lachmann in 1835 and it accounts for the passages contained in all three Gospels or in Mark and one other. (See chapter IV.) In addition to using Mark, the writers of Matthew and Luke also employed a document which is now lost, consisting mainly of the teaching of Jesus. This is generally called Q (from the first letter of the German word *Quelle*, meaning 'source') and it accounts for the parallels in Matthew and Luke. (See chapter V.) This view still leaves unaccounted for the matter found only in Matthew or in Luke.

(vi) The four-document hypothesis is an extension of the two-document theory. It accepts this but proceeds to further examination. It was first proposed by B.H. Streeter. In addition to using Mark and Q, the writer of Matthew had his own special sources or traditions, both narrative and teaching. This matter is called M. Similarly Luke's special matter, also consisting of narrative and teaching, is called L. This 'peculiar' matter in each case may have been written or oral—probably both. (See chapter VI.)

The story of Jesus is thus seen to rest, not upon three Synoptic writers (and a Johannine one) so much as upon four early sources or documents; this is shown in the following diagram.

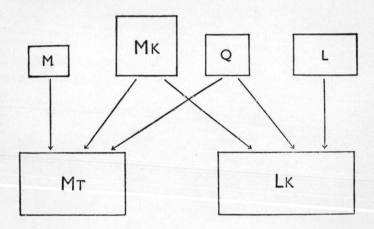

Our modern principles may be shocked at first by the suggestion that the writer of a Gospel made use of an earlier work, without acknowledging his debt. But we must remember that this was the accepted practice in ancient times. The Old Testament writers, in the historical and prophetic books, adopted this. Greek historians used sources and this practice was also followed by the Jewish historian, Josephus, in his accounts of the Jewish history and the war with Rome. There was no 'copyright' for books and no convenient signs like inverted commas or footnotes, by which a writer might show that he was quoting. An author in the first century would feel quite at liberty to make use of the work of another, sometimes copying out a paragraph with very little alteration and at other times rewriting the whole in his own style. Both these methods can be illustrated from the use of their sources by the three Synoptic evangelists.

CHAPTER IV

THE FIRST WRITTEN GOSPEL

Both the two-document theory and the four-source hypothesis, as outlined briefly towards the end of the last chapter, have as their basis the view that the Gospel of Mark was the first of the Synoptics to be written and that it was used as a main source by the writers of Matthew and Luke. This has now to be examined in detail.

REASONS FOR BELIEVING IN THE PRIORITY OF MARK

(i) Almost the whole of Mark's Gospel is found in Matthew or Luke or both. Ninety-five per cent of its total matter is contained in Matthew, while about sixty-five per cent of it is in Luke. In Mark there are 662 verses; of these, 609 have parallels in Matthew and 357 in Luke (with an additional 95 which are doubtful, as the Lukan parallel is not so exact). There are only thirty verses in Mark which have no parallel elsewhere.

(ii) The correspondence of language is striking. More than half the Greek words used in Mark are reproduced in parallel sections in the other two Gospels; in particular passages the percentage is often higher. Where Matthew or Luke diverge, Mark is generally common to one of them; there are very few cases in which Matthew and Luke agree in their language, as against Mark. In most of these instances, the two writers simply use the most natural phrasing, where Mark's is peculiar in some way.

(iii) The common order of events throughout is that of Mark. The general Synoptic outline of Jesus' life has been given in chapter III. Sometimes Matthew and sometimes Luke departs from the Markan order, but they never do so at the same point and they always return to it. The first fourteen chapters of Matthew correspond to the first six of Mark. (Matthew's total is more because the writer has included matter from other sources.) Matthew diverges from the Markan order in putting the appointment of the twelve disciples (Mark 3: 13ff) earlier (Matt. 10: 1ff), in order to introduce instruction given especially to them. The story of the 'legion' madman (Mark 5: 1–20) is put before the healing of the paralytic (Mark 2: 1–12; Matt. 8: 28ff), and the story of Jairus' daughter and the woman (Mark 5: 21–43) is inserted into the middle of the conflict stories (Matt. 9: 18–26) which are found in Mark 2. (In each case, it may be noted, the Markan order is far more likely to be the original.) The writer of Matthew, after these divergences, always returns to Mark's order. From chapter 14 onwards the order in Matthew is Mark's without any divergence in sequence of events.

Where Luke has matter parallel with Mark, in no important place does he diverge from Mark's sequence. He gives blocks of Markan matter alternating with blocks of non-Markan matter, and the Markan blocks are in the same order as they are found in Mark's Gospel. (There are a few divergences from the Markan account in matters of detail in the Passion story, but it is possible that Luke was not using Mark as his primary source there.)

Thus there is here a phenomenon similar to that observed in the matter of language. Whenever the other two writers depart from Mark, they never do so at the same point; and they always return to it, as if Mark were the common basis for their narratives.

(iv) Mark is the shortest of the three Gospels. It is far more likely that the other two made use of this brief book and expanded it with other material which was at hand, than that the writer of Mark attempted a 'cut' version of either of the others. As we have asked in chapter III, why should Mark have omitted the teaching in Matthew's Sermon on the Mount or so many of the parables of Matthew 13 or the valuable narratives and parables in Luke, such as the Prodigal Son or the Good Samaritan? It is far more reasonable to conclude that such matter was additional to Mark's original account and was inserted by a later writer.

(v) Mark's Gospel is a *relatively* simple document, when compared with the others. (This must not be taken to mean that Mark is a 'simple human biography' of Jesus, as we shall see later.) In Mark, Jesus is portrayed as the Messiah and Son of Man, and emphasis is laid upon his deeds and acts of power. There is little systematic teaching—a few parables in 4: 1–32, sayings in 9: 39–50 and an apocalyptic discourse in Chapter 13. The other two Gospels show further developments from this 'basic' portrait of Jesus and his work, Matthew seeking to emphasise the Judaistic nature of Jesus' teaching and work and Luke portraying Jesus' universal message. Each writer thus, in an opposite direction, completes the portrait which Mark, in his central position, has outlined. It is again more credible that each used Mark's account as his basis than that the writer of Mark depended on one of the others and deliberately excluded those aspects of Jesus' work and teaching which were most characteristic of his course.

(vi) When the parallel passages are studied in detail and the divergences in language are examined, we can see reasons why Matthew or Luke should have altered Mark but no reason why the reverse process should have taken place. This is seen especially in four ways:

(a) Mark's Greek style is rough-and-ready, sometimes with grammatical slips and peculiar constructions. He is fond of the present tense in narrating (in 151 instances) but he does not always keep to it in the course of a paragraph. Matthew uses this twenty-one times and Luke only once, in such passages. In Mark 11: 32 there is an unfinished sentence which dramatically breaks off with the thought of Jesus' opponents, who were muttering to themselves: 'But if we shall say, From men—they feared the people. . . .' The other two writers smooth it out: 'If we shall say, From men, we fear the multitude, (Matt. 21: 26); if we shall say from men, all the people will stone us' (Luke 20: 6). Mark tends to repeat himself. He says that tax-collectors and sinners sat down with Jesus and his disciples, and adds: 'for there were many and they followed him' (Mark 2: 15). Both Matthew and Luke omit this, as unnecessary. Mark says: 'at even, when the sun set' (1: 32). Matthew reproduces 'when even was come' (8: 16) and Luke 'when the sun was setting' (4: 40).

(b) Particular words in Mark are changed in Matthew or Luke, to make them more intelligible or acceptable to their readers. Mark sometimes gives the actual Aramaic words used by Jesus and his contemporaries in Palestine—Talitha Cumi (5: 41),

Ephphatha (7: 34), Corban (7: 11), Rabboni (10: 51), Golgotha (15: 34). Luke keeps none of the Aramaic words but substitutes Greek ones generally, while Matthew keeps only Golgotha. Mark uses a 'popular' word when he describes the pallet on which the paralytic lay (Greek *krabattos*—a poor man's mat) (Mark 2: 4, 11–12). The other two writers did not like to employ this and Matthew substituted the ordinary Greek word for 'bed' (9: 2, 6), although it would be impossible to pick up this and walk home with it. Luke likewise first describes it as a bed (5:18), then he changes it to 'couch' (5: 19, 24) and then, realising the unsuitability of these words, falls back on 'the thing he was lying on'! (5: 25). Mark, in describing Peter after his denial of Jesus, uses a colloquial expression which should probably be translated: 'He burst out weeping' or 'He set to and wept' (14: 72). Both Matthew and Luke change this to the more natural phrase, 'He went out and wept bitterly' (Matt. 26: 75; Luke 22: 62).[1]

(c) Mark's phraseology at times might give offence to Christian readers and Matthew or Luke have more acceptable phrasing, where Mark's account might imply reflection on Jesus' powers or authority. Both Matthew and Luke omit Mark's statement that some people thought Jesus was mad and that his friends (or his family) wanted to stop him from doing his work (3: 21). Mark bluntly states that at Nazareth Jesus 'could do no mighty work' (6: 5); Matthew changes this to, 'He did not do many mighty works' (13: 58). In Mark the rich man addresses Jesus as 'Good

[1] Streeter (*The Four Gospels*, p. 323) gives evidence which suggests that this is not a case of agreement of Matthew and Luke against Mark, as the words may not have been originally in Luke, Old Latin MSS. omitting them.

Master', to which Jesus responds, 'Why callest thou me good? None is good save one, God' (10: 18). Luke keeps this, but Matthew transfers the man's epithet 'good' to his question—'What good thing shall I do?'—and makes Jesus reply: 'Why askest thou me concerning that which is good?' (Matt. 19:17) and then continuing, not very suitably, with Mark: 'One there is who is good'.

In other places the narrative in Mark implies criticism of the apostles. In the storm on the Lake they arouse Jesus with the reproach: 'Master, carest thou not that we perish?' (Mark 4: 38). Matthew has: 'Save, Lord; we perish' (8: 25) and Luke: 'Master, master, we perish' (8: 24). Mark says that James and John came to Jesus demanding the chief places by his side (10: 35); Matthew spares them by saying that their mother came with the request, although she immediately drops into the background and Jesus addresses his rebuke to the men themselves, as in Mark (Matt. 20: 20ff). Mark says that the disciples were 'sore amazed' when Jesus came to them in the boat on the Lake and explains their dullness by saying that 'their hearts were hardened' (6: 51–52). Matthew says, however, that they worshipped Jesus as the son of God (14: 33). It is plain to see in these and other instances that Mark has been altered to conform with the views of later writers and to avoid giving offence to readers. The reverse process is inconceivable.

(d) Mark's narrative of particular events is often the longest of the three and it is far more likely that the accounts in Matthew and Luke are shortened versions of Mark's than that Mark has expanded either of theirs. The dramatic conversation between Jesus and the father of the epileptic boy, with its description of his fits

(Mark 9: 14–27) is briefly summarised in what we can only call Matthew's tame account (17: 14–18). Luke's is a better production (9: 38–42), but he also has omitted the central part of the story—the man's cry, 'If thou canst do anything . . .' and Jesus' rebuke. The stories of the demoniac (Mark 5: 1–20), of Jairus' daughter and the woman (5: 21–43) and the feeding of five thousand (6: 30–44) are all similarly shorter in the other two Gospels. In all these cases the others abbreviated Mark, but in doing so they deprived the story of much of its force and vivid character. The 609 verses in the whole of Mark which have parallels in Matthew are contained there in 523 verses, while the 357 verses of Mark in Luke become 325 verses.

The cumulative force of these arguments, based on extensive and exact study of the text of the three Gospels, has convinced scholars that Mark was the first of the Synoptic Gospels to be written. The reader will be able to notice further evidence for himself in studying the Gospels and comparing parallel passages.

In a copy of the New Testament the reader might indicate with a distinctive mark in the margin (say with differently coloured ink or pencil) the matter in Mark which is reproduced in Matthew or Luke only or in neither. The following are the passages:

Markan matter found only in Matthew (i.e. omitted by Luke):
1:5–6; 4: 33–34; 6: 1–6, 17–29, 45–72; 7: 5–31; 8: 1–21; 9: 10–13, 28, 43–47; 10: 1–10, 35–45; 11: 12–14, 20–22, 24; 13: 10, 18, 27, 32; 14: 26–28; 15: 3–5.
Markan matter found only in Luke (i.e. omitted by Matthew):
1: 23–28, 35–38; 4: 21–24; 6: 30; 9: 38–41; 12: 40–44.

Markan matter without any parallel in Matthew or Luke:

1: 1; 3: 20–21; 4: 26–29; 7: 3–4, 32–37; 8: 22–26; 9: 29, 48–49; 13: 33–37; 14: 51–52.

All the rest of Mark's Gospel is found in both Matthew and Luke.

MATTER PECULIAR TO MARK

It will be seen from this that there are about thirty verses in Mark which are not reproduced in either of the other two books, and each writer omits further matter. This has given rise to the question: Was the book which was used by these writers exactly the same as our Mark in its contents. It has been suggested that there existed an earlier form of Mark's Gospel (called by the German scholars *Urmarkus*, or Primitive Mark) which was shorter than our present one, without some or all of the matter not reproduced elsewhere. The great difficulty with this view is that there is no evidence that such a book existed and it is not good criticism to multiply, without very good grounds, hypothetical documents, if one can explain the facts without them.

Explanations can be better considered after examination of the passages:

(a) The matter omitted by Matthew is not of great importance. It included two stories of healing from Mark 1 (and the writer probably felt that he had enough healing stories without these) and small passages of teaching (of which also he has abundance in his Gospel, from other sources), and the story of the widow's mites.

(b) Luke omits one large section of Mark (6: 45–8: 26) and some smaller paragraphs—Jesus' visit to Nazareth

(Mark 6: 1–6), the death of John the Baptist (6: 19–29), the request of James and John (10: 35–45), a discussion with the Pharisees about divorce (10: 1–10) and the withered fig-tree (11: 12–14, 20–25), apart from short passages here and there.

(c) Both Matthew and Luke omit one parable—the growing seed (Mark 4: 26–29)—and two incidents— the healing of the deaf stammerer (7: 32–37) and the blind man at Bethsaida (8: 22–26), apart from small sections of teaching and the strange incident of the young man in Gethsemane (14: 51–52).

In most of these cases we can see good reasons why these portions of Mark should have been omitted by later writers.

(a) The parable of the growing seed would be omitted because it is so much like the parable of the mustard seed (Mark 4: 30–32), which both Matthew and Luke reproduce. It is also possible that these two writers did not favour the suggestion in the words 'the earth beareth fruit of herself' (Mark 4: 28), that the Kingdom of God flourished without human aid.

(b) The two stories of healing are in the big section of Mark which was omitted entirely by Luke (see below). Matthew omitted them probably because in both cases Jesus employed material means (saliva was thought to have healing power) and in the case of the blind man the healing was gradual, in two stages (Mark 8: 24–25). It is not strictly true to say that Matthew neglects the story of the blind man, for he has an account of two blind men (9: 27–31), in which he appears to have drawn on the story of Bartimaeus (Mark 10: 46–52) and this narrative in Mark 8.

(c) The smaller passages omitted by Luke may each be accounted for by his inclusion elsewhere of parallel matter. Instead of Mark's story of Jesus' visit to Nazareth, he gives earlier an account from another source (Luke 4: 16–30). The request of James and John, with Jesus' teaching about service, is similar to the discussion at the Last Supper (Luke 22: 24–27). The account of the withered fig-tree is anticipated in Luke by a parable about a fig-tree which bore no fruit (13: 6–9). The other two narratives were perhaps considered by him to have no interest for his Roman readers—the Jewish discussion about divorce and the somewhat gruesome account of the Baptist's death— and would be out of place in a Gentile Gospel.

(d) The omission by Luke of Mark 6: 45–8: 26 may be accounted for in one of two ways. We may take each narrative in turn and see reasons why Luke should have omitted it. The account of the walking on the Lake (Mark 6: 45–56) is like the earlier story of the storm. The discussion about Jewish rules of purity (Mark 7: 1–23) would be meaningless for Gentile readers; the conversation with the Greek woman (Mark 7: 24–30), implying a limitation of Jesus' ministry to Jews, would not be acceptable to Luke; the cure of the deaf stammerer (Mark 7: 31–37) and the blind man (8: 22–26) might remind Romans of cures by physical means by Gentile magicians; the feeding of the four thousand is so much like the five thousand that it might well be disregarded (Mark 8: 1–10); the demand of the Pharisees for a sign and the warning against them (Mark 8: 11–21) would be pointless for Gentiles. If Luke, considering the writing of a fairly lengthy book (and his Gospel is the longest of the four, as it is), had to decide to leave out something, these are the very passages which he would be most likely to omit.

An alternative explanation is that of Streeter, who conjectured that the copy of Mark's Gospel which Luke had was defective. It was torn at 6: 47 (at the words 'and he alone') and resumed at 8: 27 (with the words 'he asked his disciples'). Hence Luke puts the story of Peter's confession (without mentioning Caesarea Philippi) immediately after the feeding of the five thousand, joining these two Markan verses in the words 'as he was praying alone, the disciples were with him; and he asked them . . .' (Luke 9: 18).[1]

[1] See B. H. Streeter: *The Four Gospels*, pp. 176ff.

CHAPTER V

THE DOCUMENT Q

We now reach the next stage in the solution of the Synoptic Problem. The matter in Matthew and Luke which can be attributed to Mark accounts for over one-half of Matthew and over one-third of Luke. When we proceed to examine the non-Markan matter in these two Gospels, we are faced with further phenomena which require explanation.

NON-MARKAN PARALLELS IN MATTHEW AND LUKE

There are passages in these two books which are parallel in substance and language. Study of these prompts the question: whence did the writers obtain this material?

(i) This matter consists of about 200 verses. There are 171 verses in Matthew which are closely parallel to 151 in Luke. In addition there are over 90 verses in Matthew which have partial parallels in 94 verses in Luke. Remembering the use made of Mark as a source by the other two writers, we are led to ask: Is this another case of a common document?

(ii) In these passages the verbal agreement is often close. A very striking instance is the parable of the mote and the beam:

Matthew 7: 3–5. (3) And why beholdest thou the mote that is in thy brother's eye, but considerest not the beam that is in thine own eye? (4) Or how wilt thou say to thy brother, Let me cast out the mote out of thine eye; and lo, the beam is in thine own eye? (5) Thou hypocrite, cast out first the beam out of thine own eye; and then shalt thou see clearly to cast out the mote out of thy brother's eye.

Luke 6: 41–42 (41) And why beholdest thou the mote that is in thy brother's eye, but considerest not the beam that is in thine own eye? (42) Or how canst thou say to thy brother, Brother, let me cast out the mote that is in thine eye, when thou thyself beholdest not the beam that is in thine own eye? Thou hypocrite, cast out first the beam out of thine own eye, and then shalt thou see clearly to cast out the mote that is in thy brother's eye.

Other passages, which may be similarly set out and studied, are:

The teaching of John the Baptist:
    Matthew 3: 7–10. Luke 3: 7–9.
The temptations of Jesus:
    Matthew 4: 1–11. Luke 4: 1–12.
Teaching on anxiety:
    Matthew 6: 25–33. Luke 12: 22–31.
On confessing Christ:
    Matthew 10: 32–33. Luke 12: 8–9.
The message of John the Baptist from prison:
    Matthew 11: 2–19. Luke 7: 18–35.
The thief in the night:
    Matthew 24: 43–44. Luke 12: 39–40.

This verbal agreement again suggests a common source. As with the passages taken from Mark, the similarities are too detailed and subtle to be accounted for simply by oral tradition.

(iii) This common matter often follows the same order in the two Gospels. Each of them has a large section of Jesus' teaching (the Sermon on the Mount in Matthew 5-7, the Sermon on the Plain in Luke 6: 17-49). Both of these begin with Beatitudes and finish with the same parable; within the section the sayings on judging others and the parable given above are followed by warnings about a tree as known by its fruit and the parable of the two foundations. In both Gospels the Sermon is followed by the story of the centurion's servant (Luke 7: 1-10; Matt. 8: 5-13. Matthew inserts the Markan story of the leper first). These facts suggest not only that the section of teaching in the two accounts was in this order in a common source but also that the story of the centurion followed. Shortly afterwards, in both Gospels, there comes the account of the message of John the Baptist from prison (Matt. 11: 2-19; Luke 7: 18-35).

The conclusion drawn from a close study of all this common material is that here also Matthew and Luke were using a written document. This source has not, however, like Mark's Gospel, been preserved, so its existence must necessarily be hypothetical to a certain extent. It appears first to have been given the name of *Quelle* (German for 'Source') by Johannes Weiss in 1881, and the designation 'Q' is now generally used to indicate this matter common to Matthew and Luke but not found in Mark, or the document which contained this matter.

THE CONTENTS OF Q

This common matter consists mainly of teaching—first of John the Baptist and then of Jesus. At least two

narratives—the centurion's servant and John's message
from prison—were included. The following passages
are assigned to Q by Streeter. The order is that found
in Luke (since he reproduces Mark's order better, it
is probable that he is more to be relied on in the case
of Q also).

John the Baptist and Jesus' baptism: Luke 3: 2–9, 16–17,
  21–22. (Matt. 3: 7–12, 16–17.)
Jesus' temptations and beginning in Galilee: Luke
  4: 1–16a. (Matt. 4: 1–11.)
The Great Sermon: Luke 6: 20–49. (Matt. 5: 3, 4, 6,
  11, 12, 15, 18, 32, 39, 42–48; 6: 19–34; 7: 2–5, 7–11,
  16–27.) Many of these Matthaean passages, however, have parallels in other places in Luke, as
  shown below.
The centurion's servant: Luke 7: 1–10. (Matt. 8: 5–10,
  13.)
John's question and Jesus' opinion of John: Luke
  7: 18–35. (Matt. 11: 2–11, 16–19.)
Would-be disciples: Luke 9: 57–60 (possibly 9: 51–56,
  61–62). (Matt. 8: 19–22.)
The mission of disciples: Luke 10: 2–16, 21–24. (Matt.
  9: 37–38; 10: 10–13, 16; 11: 25–27; 13: 16–17.)
Jesus' defence against the Beelzebub charge: Luke
  11: 9–52. (Matt. 7: 7–11; 12: 22–27, 38–45; 5: 15;
  6: 22–23; 23 (passim).)
Warnings against fears and cares: Luke 12: 1a–12,
  22–59. (Matt. 10: 26–33; 12: 32; 6: 19–21, 25–33;
  24: 43–51; 10: 34–36; 5: 25–26.)
Parables of the mustard seed and the leaven: Luke
  13: 18–21. (Matt. 13: 31–33.)
Sayings about entrance into the Kingdom: Luke
  13: 22–30. (Matt. 7: 13; 8: 11–12.)

The lament over Jerusalem: Luke 13: 34–35. (Matt. 23: 37–39.)

Warnings to disciples: Luke 14: 11, 26–27, 34–35. (Matt. 10: 37–38; 5: 13.)

The Law and divorce: Luke 16: 13, 16–18. (Matt. 6: 24; 11: 12–13; 5: 18, 32.)

Warnings against stumbling-blocks, etc: Luke 17: 1–6, 20–37. (Matt. 18: 6–7, 15, 21–22; 17: 20; 24 (passim).)

Possibly three parables where the parallels are not so close:

The Great Supper (or Marriage Feast): Luke 14: 15–24. (Matt. 22: 1–10.)

The Lost Sheep: Luke 15: 3–7. (Matt. 18: 12–14.)

The Pounds (or Talents): Luke 19: 12–27. (Matt. 25: 14–30.)

In the reader's copy of the Gospels there might now be indicated, by colours in the margin, the Q matter in Matthew and Luke.

The contents of Q might be classified as follows:

(i) John the Baptist and the baptism and temptations of Jesus.

(ii) The teaching of Jesus to his followers—warnings against fears and anxiety, against causing stumbling; the charge to the disciples when they were sent out on their mission.

(iii) Parables—the mustard seed and the leaven; possibly others.

(iv) Jesus' conflict with his opponents; sayings about the Jewish Law; warnings to would-be disciples.

(v) Two narratives—the centurion's servant and John's message from prison.

The material from Q contains many of Jesus' references to the countryside and the processes of nature. It portrays the more human side of Jesus' personality and work. There is little about Judaism or teaching that would be of special interest to Jewish disciples. This suggests that Q was compiled for a church which was largely Gentile. This may have been Antioch, where, according to the Acts of the Apostles (11: 20), the first preaching was made to the Greeks.

It is probable that Q was compiled before Mark's Gospel and so it is one of the earliest writings of the Church. But it would be a mistake to regard it as a complete Gospel. There is no suggestion, for instance, that Q contained an account of the Passion. The matter in Matthew and Luke which we may assign to Q ceases when Jesus reaches Jerusalem. Both Matthew and Luke diverge when they give information additional to Mark's account of the last days in Jerusalem. It is possible that Luke based his narrative on another source, but Matthew follows Mark from his chapter 21 onwards quite closely, and if there had been a Passion story in Q he would surely have made use of it to supplement Mark's account, as he does in so many of the earlier Markan narratives. But in the Passion narrative his additional matter comes from his own special source, which is not at all comparable with Q in tone or in reliability.

It is, however, probable that Q was longer than we can gauge simply from the parallel matter in Matthew and Luke. Some of the passages which are peculiar to either may well have come from Q but ignored for some reason by the other writer. Thus Matthew has Jesus' reply to two would-be disciples (8: 19–22), found also in Luke (9: 57–60). But Luke adds a reply to a

E

third man (9: 61–62), which may well have been in Q
also. Of Matthew's parables of the Kingdom of God
in chapter 13, two are assigned to Q (the mustard
seed and the leaven), for they are paralleled in Luke,
but possibly the parables of the treasure and the pearl-
merchant (Matt. 13: 44–46) were also taken by him
from Q. If we may judge from their use of Mark, it is
very unlikely that either writer made use of the whole
of Q and quite probable that one of them has reproduced it more fully than the other.

Some critics have consequently suggested two
editions of Q. They might be called Q (Matt.) and
Q (Luke); the contents of each edition might be considered to include all the non-Markan matter in
Matthew and Luke respectively. But these two documents would be so unlike each other in their total
extent that it would hardly be proper to call them a
common source. It is safer to keep the symbol Q for
the matter which is strictly parallel.

THE ORIGINAL FORM OF Q

When we examine the Markan matter in Matthew
and Luke, we find it is Luke who keeps to the order of
the narrative better than Matthew. It is therefore
probable that the order of the passages from Q is
nearer the original in Luke. Luke further tends to
reproduce blocks of Q matter, alternating with blocks
of Markan matter. But Matthew is fond of conflating
his sources, mixing up Markan material and passages
from Q and elsewhere, so that it is very difficult to
disentangle them in his finished Gospel. It is much
easier to extract Q matter from Luke.

We are not on such sure ground when we consider

the question of the original wording of Q. We must
bear in mind the free way in which both the other
writers treated Mark's Gospel, Matthew abbreviating
and sometimes omitting quite vital matter in a narrative
and Luke re-writing Markan passages in his own style.
It is probable, therefore, that they treated Q in much
the same way. It seems sometimes as if one writer and
sometimes the other gives the original words of Q.
Did Q have 'How wilt thou say . . .?' (Matt. 7: 4) or
'How canst thou say . . .?' (Luke 6: 42)? Did it read,
'You shall be perfect, as your heavenly Father is
perfect' (Matt. 5: 48) or 'Be merciful, even as your
Father is merciful' (Luke 6: 36)? Is the poetic form of
the parable of the two foundations (in Matt. 7: 24–27)
the original, of which Luke made a prose version
(Luke 6: 47–49), or is Luke's prose the original, which
Matthew set out in the form of Semitic poetry?

The original language of Q has also given rise to
discussion. Jesus spoke in Aramaic and his teaching
would be first repeated in that language, among Jewish
disciples. Was Q originally written in Aramaic? If it
was, it is probable that it had already been translated
into Greek, before it was used by the two Synoptics.
Luke, at any rate, would probably know no Aramaic,
and would use the Greek document; and it is likely
also that the writer of Matthew combined a Greek Q
with the Greek Mark. But it is possible that they did
not use the same Greek translation and this might
account for some of the divergences in their wording.
There is a hint of such in at least one passage. Luke
has the strange phrase, 'Give for alms those things
which are within' (11: 41), while Matthew has
'Cleanse the inside of the cup' (23: 26). Matthew seems
obviously to be correct, but how did the strange

language of Luke arise? Wellhausen pointed out that
the Aramaic for 'give alms' is *zakki*, while for 'cleanse'
it is *dakki*. The Greek translator whose work Luke used
misread *dakki* as *zakki* (and the initial letters are very
similar in the Hebrew characters in which Aramaic
was written).

MARK AND Q

There are some places where Mark and Q overlapped. There are about forty verses in Mark which
are also found in a similar form in Matthew and Luke
where (as can be seen particularly clearly in Luke) the
context is Q matter. Hence we are justified in assigning
them to Q as well as Mark. The passages in Mark
which are thus paralleled are:

Mark 1: 4–8: John the Baptist's preaching.
Mark 1: 9–13: The baptism and temptation of Jesus.
Mark 3: 22–30: The accusation of Jesus' enemies.
Mark 4: 30–32: The parable of the mustard seed.
Mark 6: 7–11: The mission of the twelve disciples.
Mark 12: 38–40: Warning against the scribes.
Various short sayings: 4: 21 (the lamp); 8: 12 (the
    demand for a sign); 8: 34 (taking up the cross); 8: 38
    (being ashamed of Christ); 9: 42 (on causing to
    stumble); 9: 50 (on salt); 10: 11 (divorce); 11: 22–23
    (on faith); 13: 21 (false Messiahs).

The question inevitably arises: Did Mark make use
of Q? Opinion on this question has been divided among
scholars, but it is generally concluded today that Mark
did not know of or did not use Q. If this document had
been available to him, he would surely have reproduced

not merely these few short passages but more of the teaching of Jesus. The wording in Mark and Q also is not generally near enough to suggest Mark's use of the same source as Matthew and Luke in these places. The occurrence of passages in both Mark and Q indicates that some of the teaching of Jesus was remembered and written down independently in different places. The fact that both Mark and the compiler of Q (and subsequently the writers of Matthew and Luke) included these particular passages is an argument for their dependability as genuine teaching of Jesus.

CHAPTER VI

MATTER PECULIAR TO MATTHEW AND LUKE

When we have extracted from Matthew and Luke the
Markan material and the passages taken from Q, we
are still left with a considerable amount of matter found
only in the one Gospel in each case. This matter is
generally designated, for convenience, M and L
respectively.

MATTER PECULIAR TO MATTHEW

This consists of 282 verses. In addition, there are
about 90 verses which have partial parallels in Luke;
we cannot be certain whether they come from Q or
should be classed with this M material. The matter
peculiar to Matthew consists of narratives, of additions
made to the Markan account and of teaching of Jesus.

(i) Narratives found only in Matthew are: The
genealogy of Jesus and stories of his birth and infancy
(chaps. 1–2), the healing of two blind men (9: 27–31;
this, however, seems to be a conflation of Mark 8: 22–26
and 10: 46–52), the coin in the fish's mouth (17: 24–27),
the end of Judas (28: 3–10), the guard at the tomb
(27: 62–66; 28: 11–15), the resurrection appearance
in Galilee (28: 16–20).

(ii) The main additions to the Markan narratives
are: The hesitation of John at the baptism (3: 13),

Jesus' preaching in Galilee, with an Old Testament quotation (4: 13–16), teaching in the incident in the cornfields (12: 5–7), healing by Jesus, with an Old Testament quotation (12: 15–21), the people's question about Jesus as Son of David (12: 23), Peter's attempt to walk on the water (14: 28–31), additions to the story of the Greek woman (15: 22–25), the praise and promise to Peter at Caesarea Philippi (16: 17–19), details in the story of the entry into Jerusalem, including an Old Testament quotation (21: 4–5), healing and praise of Jesus in the Temple (21: 14–16), Judas' reply at the Last Supper (26: 25), Jesus' words at his arrest (26: 52–53), the warning of Pilate's wife (27: 19), Pilate's hand-washing (27: 24–25), the earthquake at the crucifixion (27: 51–53), the descent of an angel and an earthquake at the tomb (28: 3–4).

(iii) The teaching of Jesus found only in Matthew consists of:

Sections of the Sermon on the Mount (5: 7–10, 13–24, 27–30, 33–48; 6: 1–18; 7: 13–23).

Parts of the charge to the disciples (10: 5–8, 23–25, 40–41).

Most of chapter 23 (Woes on the Pharisees and scribes).

Ten parables: The tares (13: 24–30, 36–43), the hidden treasure (13: 44), the pearl merchant (13: 45–46), the drag-net (13: 47–50), the unforgiving servant (18: 21–35), the labourers in the vineyard (20: 1–16), the two sons (21: 28–31a), the man without a wedding garment (22: 11–14), the ten maidens at the wedding (25: 1–13), the sheep and the goats (25: 31–46). There are three parables which have partial parallels in Luke: the lost sheep (Matt. 18: 12–14), the marriage feast (22: 1–10), the talents (25: 14–30).

Various sayings: 9: 13a; 11: 28; 12: 5–7, 11–12; 13: 52; 15: 22b–24; 18: 15–22; 19: 28.

Much of this M material gives Matthew's Gospel its distinctive tone. The narratives are characterised by references to angels and dreams as means of divine revelation, and there is a tendency to heighten the miraculous and the marvellous. Quotations from the Old Testament and Jewish phrases are inserted into the narrative, sometimes quite unsuitably. Matter relating to Peter is added to Mark's accounts. Some of the material raises suspicions as to its historicity and borders on the apocryphal.

The teaching of Jesus in M brings out the Jewish element in the gospel, in Jesus' attitude towards the Law and the anti-Pharisaic tone of many of the sayings. There is an interest in eschatology and judgment and an emphasis on the Church. These characteristics of Matthew's Gospel will be further considered in chapter IX.

MATTER PECULIAR TO LUKE

This consists of about 490 verses, to which we might add material which may have come from Q, as there are partial parallels in Matthew. It comprises both narative and teaching.

(i) The narratives found only in Luke are: The stories of the birth of John the Baptist and Jesus (1: 5 to 2: 40), the incident of Jesus' boyhood (2: 41–52), the genealogy of Jesus (4: 23–38), the rejection at Nazareth (4: 16–30), the call of Peter (5: 1–11), the widow's son at Nain (7: 11–17), the anointing in Simon's house (7: 36–50), the women who accompanied

Jesus (8: 1–3), the Samaritan village rejection (9: 51–56), a would-be disciple (9: 61–62), the return of seventy disciples (10: 17–20), Mary and Martha (10: 38–42), the healing of an infirm woman (13: 10–17), the plot of Herod (13: 31), the healing of a man with dropsy (14: 1–6), the healing of ten lepers (17: 11–19), the meeting with Zacchaeus (19: 1–10), the lament over Jerusalem (19: 41–44), a quarrel at the Last Supper and words to Peter (22: 24–34), the trial before Pilate (in some details) and Herod Antipas (23: 1–25), the weeping of the Jerusalem women (23: 27–31), the two crucified criminals (23: 39–43), the walk to Emmaus (24: 13–35), the appearances of Jesus in Jerusalem and the ascension (24: 36–53).

(ii) The teaching matter found only in Luke consists of: Various sayings: 4: 25–27 (Jesus' address at Nazareth); 12: 13–15 (warnings about riches); 13: 1–5 (the Galilaeans and the Siloam tower); 13: 31–33 (Jesus on Herod); 14: 7–14 (on inviting to a banquet); 16: 14–15 (on the Pharisees); 22: 24–30 (on greatness and service); 23: 34, 43, 46 (sayings at the crucifixion). Other passages, not attributable to Jesus: 1: 1–4 (the dedication to Theophilus); 3: 10–14, 15, 17 (John the Baptist's teaching).

There are fourteen parables peculiar to Luke: The two debtors (7: 41–42), the good Samaritan (10: 30–37), the friend at midnight (11: 5–8), the foolish rich man (12: 15–21), the fig tree (13: 6–9), the tower builder (14: 28–30), the king going to war (14: 31–32), the lost coin (15: 8–10), the prodigal son (15: 11–32), the unrighteous steward (16: 1–12), the rich man and Lazarus (16: 19–31), the slave and his master (17: 7–10), the unjust judge (18: 1–8), the Pharisee and tax-collector (18: 10–14). Three parables have a partial parallel in Matthew: The great supper (14: 15-24), the lost sheep (15: 3-7), the pounds (19: 12-27).

As in the case of Matthew, it is here also that this special matter gives the characteristic tone to the whole Gospel. The narratives show an interest in women, in outcasts and Samaritans and in Roman officials. The teaching of Jesus emphasises prayer, the Spirit of God, women and outcasts. (See also chapter X.)

The matter peculiar to each Gospel could be marked in the reader's New Testament with a special colour for each. If matter from Q has already been marked in a distinctive way, the sections in Matthew and Luke without any indication will be those taken from Mark.

THE FORM OF THIS MATERIAL

In view of the previous study of Mark and Q, as well as the researches of the Form-Critics, the question arises: Was the matter peculiar to one Gospel taken from a written source or did the writer simply reproduce the oral material in these passages? It is difficult to say with certainty in either case.

(a) In the case of Matthew's M matter, one of the sources was probably a collection of Old Testament passages, already arranged in writing. At points in his narrative he introduces these, sometimes suitably but frequently in a forced and artificial way. This suggests that he did not quote these direct from the Old Testament (and some of them do not agree in wording with either the Hebrew or a Greek version) but made use of a collection of passages which he had at hand.

The way in which the teaching in Matthew is

arranged also frequently suggests the use of a written document—for instance the five examples of Jesus' attitude to the Law (5: 17–48) and the three instances of Jewish religious observance (6: 1–18). Similarly the three parables of judgment in chapter 25 may already have been arranged in this way in written form. Some of this arrangement may, however, be due to the skill of the writer of Matthew; we have an example of this in chapter 13, where he has augmented Mark 4 with other material, from Q and M, to compile a collection of parables. The connected piece of denunciation of the Pharisees in Matthew 23 likewise consists of material from Q and M, put together by the writer himself.

The narratives peculiar to Matthew were probably oral traditions which circulated in a Jewish Christian environment. They are mostly fragmentary in nature—details about Peter or Pilate or Judas which the writer thought fit to introduce into his account; there is little extended continuous narrative, apart from the birth-stories of chapters 1 and 2. Some of the matter introduced into the Markan narratives consists simply of editorial comments.

(b) Luke's peculiar narrative matter may have been written down beforehand or may be oral stories which he himself heard. If the author was the companion of Paul, who stayed with him at Jerusalem and Caesarea (Acts 21–26), the latter is more likely. But if the author was a later writer, it is more likely that he found written accounts of at least some of these stories. In either case, he re-wrote them in his own Greek style.

The teaching peculiar to Luke consists mainly of parables; the sayings enumerated above are often given in connection with parables or incidents. One feature of the Lukan parables is that they are placed in a particular setting in many instances and sometimes have a fairly long narrative introduction—e.g. the two debtors (7: 36ff), the good Samaritan (10: 25ff), the foolish rich man (12: 13ff), the lost sheep and coin (15: 1ff), the pounds (19: 11ff). Sometimes the Lukan setting seems somewhat artificial and the parables could well stand by themselves; for instance, by the time the third of the parables of the 'lost' is reached (15: 11ff), the original situation in 15: 1–2 has been lost sight of. These facts suggest that at least in some cases the parable may have existed separately, perhaps in a written collection, and has been placed in this setting by Luke.

ANALYSIS AND SYNTHESIS OF THE GOSPEL MATERIAL

The study pursued so far has been analytic. We have split up the Gospels into their constituent elements, noticing their sources and how they were compiled. Evidence has been examined in favour of the two-source theory and the four-document hypothesis. The summary and the diagram shown at the close of chapter III will now be appreciated with fuller understanding.

The next stage is synthetic. We have to see each of the Gospels as an entity, to study the characteristics of each, to see the aims and methods of the writer and to appreciate the full effect of his finished work.

CHAPTER VII

THE GOSPEL OF MARK:
(1) ITS CONSTRUCTION AND PURPOSE

THE CONSTRUCTION OF THE GOSPEL

Mark's Gospel, as the first of our four, was probably the first attempt to set down an account of the life and work of Jesus in an orderly and systematic form. The main sources used by the writer were in all probability oral. He knew the episodes which we have classified as Pronouncement-stories, miracle-stories, biographical-sketches, and the teaching of Jesus which was reported among the early Christians. If some of it was already written down (a point which is discussed in the next chapter), it would probably be of a fragmentary character.

The material at his disposal was arranged by the author to form a 'book'. In making his selection of episodes and teaching, he put together material which had a similar subject or purpose. He thus gave an account of (a) activities connected with the opening of Jesus' ministry in Galilee (chapter 1); (b) stories of conflict with the Jewish authorities (2–3); (c) parables illustrative of Jesus' teaching (4); (d) acts of power (5); (e) the training of disciples (6) and journeys outside Galilee (7–9); (f) a journey to Jerusalem (10); (g) the last days in Jerusalem (11–16). This constitutes the Markan 'scheme' which, as we have seen, was largely followed by Matthew and Luke.

THE CHARACTERISTICS OF MARK'S GOSPEL

The writer made most use of the accounts of Jesus' activities. In this book there is an impression of speed and urgency. The writer is fond of the Greek word translated 'straightway' or 'immediately'. He goes from one incident to another with very little 'padding' in between. He crowds a large amount of activity into his very first chapter. He is fond of the historic present tense, using it 151 times in his narrative. The book opens without formal introduction, with an abrupt statement about John the Baptist, prefaced by what appears to be a kind of 'heading'—'The beginning of the gospel . . . .' Jesus appears, without previous introduction, at verse 9. The style of the Greek is rough and the grammar sometimes faulty.

Mark presents three aspects of the life and person of Jesus:

(i) As a man of action and of mighty works. From the first, Jesus' authority is noticed by the people—in his words (1: 22) and in his deeds (1: 27; cf. 2: 12). The author seems to be answering, by anticipation, the question which Jesus' enemies put to him: 'By what authority doest thou these things?' (11: 28). Mark regards the powers of Jesus as a demonstration of his divine mission and his Messiahship.

(ii) As the Messiah. This is the 'heading' of the book (1: 1). The demons recognize this (1: 24, 34), but it is not known by men. They think of him only as John the Baptist or Elijah or a prophet (8: 28). Peter's acknowledgment at Caesarea Philippi (8: 29) marks a turning-point in the narrative. Jesus is first publicly proclaimed as Messiah by Bartimaeus at Jericho (10: 47). The Messiahship is hinted at on the occasion of his entry into Jerusalem (11: 9–10) but the first claim to that dignity by Jesus himself is at his trial, in answer to a question from the High Priest (14: 61–62). The book closes with the verdict of the Roman centurion, that this was 'a son of God' (15: 39)—meant by him no doubt in a pagan way but intended by Mark to be understood in the Christian sense.

(iii) As the Servant. After Caesarea Philippi (8: 31ff) Jesus speaks of a suffering Messiah, who serves and sacrifices himself for men. Three times there is a forecast of what will happen at Jerusalem (8: 31; 9: 31; 10: 33). The thought of the Messiah seems to be combined with the conception of the Suffering Servant, as pictured by Deutero-Isaiah; but the term used is 'Son of Man'; apart from 2: 10 and 2: 28 (of which varying explanations have been given), this term occurs only after Caesarea Philippi. There appears to be a definite reminiscence of Isaiah 53 in the words given in 10: 45, that 'the Son of Man came not to be served but to serve, and to give his life a ransom for many'.

(iv) As a teacher. Much of the teaching in Mark is given in connection with incidents or in answer to questions from disciples or enemies. Many of the Pronouncement-stories, ending with a saying of Jesus, are found in Mark. More specific and connected teaching is given in the parables in 4: 3–34, the sayings in 9: 41–50 and the apocalyptic chapter 13.

DIFFERENT VIEWS OF MARK'S GOSPEL

Students of Mark have shown great divergence in their views of the nature of the book and what it is intended to teach.

(i) One traditional way of regarding the Gospel has been to treat its outline as a reliable account, in detail, of the ministry of Jesus, correct in its chronology and the order of events, preserving genuine reminiscence of the disciples. It is this outline, as we have seen above (p. 29), which is followed in the main by the other two Synoptists. The 'Markan hypothesis', as it was called, sought to trace this definite 'scheme' in the account, as evidence of careful planning and exact reporting on the part of Mark.

In the Galilaean period, Mark includes stories of Jesus' preaching, healing acts and opposition from his enemies which, in contrast to the general popularity, his words and works evoked. The 'Galilaean sunshine' was also clouded by misunderstanding at Nazareth. So Jesus chose twelve men to be with him and learn his secret and to go forth to preach his message. Jesus had decided not to trust the great crowds but to concentrate on a few. On the return of these apostles from their mission tour, Jesus wished for retirement with them, but was frustrated by the crowds, when he crossed the lake, and was discovered even by a Greek woman in Phoenicia. So he proceeded to Herod Philip's territory and there, away from the crowds, the disciples reported on their work and on people's views about Jesus and Peter made his confession. Thereafter Jesus began to speak of a suffering Messiah and shortly afterwards the journey to Jerusalem (apparently the only one) commenced, leading swiftly to the final clash with the Jewish authorities there and the crucifixion.

There is admittedly much that is attractive in this view and it gives an intelligible and straightforward story of Jesus' ministry. It was generally assumed by

the supporters of this view that this outline came from
Peter, who was thus the writer's informant not only
about particular incidents but also the general order
of events throughout.

This view, however, has its difficulties. The Markan
'scheme' is incomplete and inadequate chronologically.
There is little indication of the passing of time in Mark;
the only mention of the seasons of the year is in the
references to the ears of corn in 2: 23 and the green
grass in 6: 39, both of which indicate the spring. But
we have no clue whether it is the same spring or whether
that was the year in which Jesus went to Jerusalem. If
all the events in Mark's story happened within twelve
months, is that enough for Jesus to have become known
throughout Galilee and even for his fame to have
reached Phoenicia (7: 24) and Jericho (10: 47)?
Mark records only one visit to Jerusalem, whereas Q
hints that he had more than once appealed to the city
(Luke 13: 34; Matt. 23: 37: 'How often . . .'). This
document also suggests an extensive ministry in places
in Galilee which are either mentioned only once in
Mark (e.g. Bethsaida: Mark 8: 22) or not mentioned
at all (e.g. Chorazin: Luke 10: 13; Matt. 11: 21).
When Jesus reaches Jerusalem, there is no indication
in Mark how long it was before the Passion; the popular
view of a 'Holy week' is based on the assumption that
the entry into the city took place on a 'Sunday',
but Mark does not say so. It might have happened
some time before the Passover. The only indication of
time in the Jerusalem period is the note that the plot
against Jesus was hatched two days before the Passover (Mark 14: 1).

It is indeed perilous to rely upon Mark for an
adequate or chronological outline of Jesus' work. It

F

is doubtful if Mark would have been interested in this, even if he had been able to provide it. He was concerned to set forth a gospel—a proclamation of good news (1: 1). This is not to say that his outline of Jesus' ministry is unreliable. On the whole it presents a true historical picture of Galilaean work, healing and teaching, the opposition of his enemies, his journey to Jerusalem and the last days. But we must not claim for it more than the writer himself intended. It is going too far to conclude that the general 'scheme' of Mark represents a fully trustworthy and carefully worked-out account, covering all the incidents narrated, so that it is possible to say of an incident that it happened at a particular place at a particular stage in the ministry.

(ii) The Form Critics go to the other extreme and tend to regard Mark as a kind of patchwork, without the possibility of placing any reliability on its historical and geographical notices. It embodies the oral material which was in circulation in the early Church, but the writer had at hand only fragmentary and disconnected episodes. They hold that the connections between the paragraphs are entirely artificial, being the work of Mark himself, and are not to be depended on to give any reliable account of the situation or the connection between different incidents.

The truth in this view is that the Gospel is certainly a collection of episodes and there are abrupt transitions between one paragraph and another; sometimes there does seem to be little relation between consecutive paragraphs. But it is going too far to suggest that no reliance can be placed on the Markan arrangement. There is definite progression in Mark's account; the ministry of Jesus begins after his baptism by John and his temptations; his main work is done in Galilee;

thence he travels to Jerusalem, where the opposition of the Jewish authorities reaches its climax. The writer is here surely following a tradition of the course of Jesus' work, although in but general terms, and he has arranged his oral material within this historical framework.

The view of the Gospel as a series of disconnected episodes without any trustworthy or certain connection thus goes too far in the other direction, as a revolt against the rigidity of the 'Markan hypothesis'.

(iii) Mark is often regarded to-day primarily as a theological work. It is held by such critics—although from many differing points of view—that Mark did not intend to give an objective narrative of the life and work of Jesus; his book is neither a history nor a biography but is the writing of a theologian. The first attempt must be to understand his theological point of view; then his treatment of the story of Jesus becomes plain. A number of such recent views can only be summarised here:

(a) W. Wrede in 1901 (in a book which has never been translated into English—*Das Messiasgeheimnis in den Evangelien*) produced a theory that Mark's Gospel was written in order to expound a theory of the 'Messianic secret'. Faced with the fact that the early Christians proclaimed Jesus as the Messiah after the resurrection, Wrede said that this was their own invention and that Jesus was not accepted as the Messiah until then and did not himself claim to be the Messiah. The Gospel of Mark was written to account for the Christian proclamation, in face of Jesus' own silence. The writer held that Jesus was recognized as Messiah by the demons, and later by the intimate band of disciples, but he told them to keep this a secret until after the resurrection. The 'Messianic secret' was, however, so Wrede urged, an artificial construction, and the Gospel was the exposition of a theological view, not to be regarded as historically reliable.

(b) A different point of view was upheld by J. H. Ropes, who regarded Mark's Gospel as 'a kind of theological pamphlet', which was written to explain how it was that the Messiah suffered death at the hands of his own people. 'The Gospel of Mark is a discussion of a theological problem in the form of a dramatic historical sketch.'[1]

(c) Others have held that the writer of Mark was a Paulinist and was concerned mainly to expound the views of the apostle to the Gentiles. Paul deals in Rom. 9–11 with the problem of the rejection of the Messiah; the counterpart of this teaching, so B. W. Bacon held, is the theory in Mark of the 'hardening' of the disciples' hearts (Mark 6: 52; 8: 17).[2] Loisy advanced this idea of Paul's influence on the writer of Mark to the extreme of holding that Paul himself is referred to in the 'outsider' with whose work the original disciples were not to interfere (Mark 9: 38–40) and the 'little one' who must be received in Jesus' name (Mark 9: 37).[3]

(d) A more recent attempt to understand Mark in this theological way is that of Austin Farrer, who holds that Mark's theological arrangement was cyclic. The narratives told in the early parts of the book 'prefigure' the later events of the Passion and resurrection. He holds that this restores the unity of the Gospel and makes it 'a profoundly consistent, complex act of

---

[1] *The Synoptic Gospels*, p. 12.
[2] *The Gospel of Mark*, p. 144. *Is Mark a Roman Gospel?* p. 80.
[3] *L'Evangile selon Marc*, pp. 279f.

thought'. The book is consequently arranged not on an historical basis but artificially, as determined by 'motives of Christian symbolism'.[1]

The 'theological' view of Mark has arisen to a large extent as a reaction against the view that the book presented a 'simple human Jesus', in contrast to the other Gospels, and was to be treated as a straightforward biography. It does seem plain now that much of the arrangement of Mark's material is due to the writer himself and that doctrinal considerations did influence him in this. But one suspects that in some cases the critic is reading into Mark's narrative theological conclusions which he has himself reached on other grounds.

Another difficulty is that the critics are by no means agreed on what was the theological purpose of Mark and their views are often divergent and irreconcilable. There is much in the Gospel, too, which plainly has no connection with a theological purpose; many of the incidents are surely related simply because the writer thought it worth while to preserve them and to give them a more permanent form than they could ever have had in the oral period.

[1] *A Study in St. Mark*, pp. 7, 146.

CHAPTER VIII

THE GOSPEL OF MARK:
(2) ITS SOURCES AND AUTHORSHIP

THE SOURCES OF MARK'S GOSPEL

In the case of Matthew and Luke, we have seen how we can trace the use of written sources and can say of a certain passage from which document or tradition it was taken. In the case of Mark the study is necessarily more uncertain and speculative, as there has not been preserved any previous attempt at the writing of a Gospel, of which Mark may have made use.

(i) One source was obviously the oral material which we have studied in chapter II. Many of Mark's narratives still bear the marks of the 'form' which they took when still being told by word of mouth. The study of Form-Criticism is generally concerned mainly with Mark's Gospel.

(ii) The oldest tradition about the authority behind Mark is contained in the words of Papias, who was bishop of Hierapolis, in Asia Minor, about A.D. 130. As reported by Eusebius, the Church historian (about 325), Papias quotes 'the Elder' (or 'Presbyter') as saying: 'Mark, having become the interpreter of Peter, wrote down accurately all that he remembered of the things said and done by the Lord, but not however in order. For neither did he hear the Lord, nor did he follow him, but afterwards, as I said, (attached himself) to Peter, who adapted his teaching to the needs

(of the moment, or: of his hearers), but not as though
he were drawing up a connected account of the Lord's
sayings. So then Mark made no mistake in thus record-
ing some things just as he remembered them, for he
made it his one care to omit nothing that he had heard
and to make no false statement in them.'

According to this statement, the authority behind
Mark was Peter. The word 'interpreter' has sometimes
been taken to mean that Mark translated Peter's words
from one language to another—perhaps from Peter's
Aramaic to the common Greek. It is, however, more
likely that the word means rather a kind of secretary
or one who sought to interpret Peter's ideas to others.
If the writer is John Mark of the Acts, his relation to
Peter might be the same as he had formerly had towards
Paul and Barnabas (Acts 13: 5).

Most students of Mark have concluded that there is
Petrine matter in Mark and that the authority of the
apostle lies in some measure behind the book. Peter is
especially mentioned in such places as 1: 30; 9: 5; 10: 28;
11: 21; 16: 7 (apart from passages where he naturally
plays a leading role). C. H. Turner has suggested that
in many of the narratives the third person plural which
begins a paragraph ('they come . . .' etc.—1: 21, 29;
9: 33; 10: 32; 11: 27) might well represent what was
originally a first person plural, as the stories were told
by Peter ('we come . . .', etc.).

The reference which Papias makes to Mark's 'order'
has sounded to some students to be disparaging. Some
have concluded that the Elder was comparing Mark's
chronological scheme with some other 'order' in
another book—perhaps the Gospel of Matthew or the
Fourth Gospel, which certainly does give a different
'order' in several respects. Others have taken the word

to refer rather to literary arrangement; in this case the comparison is more likely to have been with Matthew, where the author has arranged Jesus' teaching in particular in a more orderly fashion. P. Carrington, however, holding that Mark was compiled to provide lessons for reading in Christian services, considers that Papias was criticising Mark's calendrical order, as an arrangement of lections, because this could not be used, or could only be used with difficulty, in the Asiatic churches with which he was concerned.[1] It is, however, possible that all these views read too much into Papias' words and that he was referring in general terms to the lack of connection between incidents in the Gospel and the fact that the arrangement of similar material is not consistently carried through in the whole book.

(iii) Petrine matter does not, however, account for the whole Gospel. There are traits which do not suggest an eye-witness behind the narrative. There are two accounts of the feeding of a multitude (6: 34–44; 8: 1–10), which are generally considered to be variants of the same incident. The second—the feeding of four thousand—is probably not so reliable as the first. This suggests that Mark had two different accounts, from more than one source; one may have been oral and the other written. The confusion which is shown in some places about the geography of Galilee and the north of Palestine in general also suggests that the writer had not at hand an eye-witness, to whom he could refer for more accurate details.

(iv) It is probable that some written sources were used for the teaching of Jesus in Mark. The parables in 4: 3–34 may already have been written down and

[1] *The Primitive Christian Calender*, pp. 58f.

arranged in this fashion. There is a series of sayings in 9: 41–50, which are introduced by an incident (9: 38–40), but there is little connection between this and the sayings which follow or indeed between sayings which are here put together. The connecting links seem to consist of words which occur in contiguous sayings, such as 'name' (verses 39 and 41: see the R.V. margin for the literal rendering here), 'cause to stumble' (verses 42 and 43–47), 'fire' (verses 48–49) and 'salt' (verses 49–50). This suggests that the sayings were already collected and Mark simply copied them into his Gospel. Such a document would be somewhat like Q, although a quite independent collection.

It is probable also that a written document underlies chapter 13 or part of it. This chapter consists of teaching of Jesus said to have been given to the three chosen apostles, in answer to a question about the time of the destruction of the Temple (13: 1–3). But most of the chapter has little relation to this initial enquiry and consists of the 'signs' and other features which were common in apocalyptic thought and literature among Jews and Christians in the first century. It has often been thought that Mark was making use of a written document in this chapter, compiled by some Jewish-Christian writer. This 'Little Apocalypse', as it is called, may have consisted of verses 7–8, 14–20 and 24–27, which reflect the conventional apocalyptic outlook more than the rest of the chapter. To this some writer—perhaps Mark himself—added warnings which Jesus gave to the disciples about the treatment which they must expect from men and exhortations to watch for some coming crisis. The theory of the Little Apocalypse is not held now so rigidly as it was once; but it is still possible that verses 5–27 had already been compiled and were inserted by Mark into his narrative at this point.

(v) In recent years attempts have been made to distinguish a number of written sources, both for Mark's narrative matter and the teaching. Vincent Taylor draws attention to what he calls a number of 'small complexes'—groups of narratives in which there is a common theme or interest, such as the stories of cures in 1: 21–39, the conflict stories in 2: 1–3: 6, the parables in 4: 1–34, the statements about ritual cleanness in 7: 1–23 and the incidents on the journey through Perea in 10: 1–31.[1] Some of these may have already existed in written form before Mark included them in his Gospel.

More elaborate attempts have been made to identify Mark's sources and even their authors. E. Wendling (1905) held that there were three strata discernible in the finished Gospel, due respectively to the hand of an historian, a poet and a theologian. Edward Meyer (1921) distinguished one source in which 'the disciples' are prominent and another in which they are called 'the twelve'. A. T. Cadoux (1935) discovered three completed Gospels which were brought together to form our Mark—an early Palestinian Gospel, written for Jews, translated from Aramaic about A.D. 40, another for the Jews of the dispersion written in Greek about 66 and a later one for Gentiles, written in Rome.[2] For J. M. C. Crum (1936), on the other hand, the whole book, as he studied it, 'came in two' and 'the one Mark became two Marks'.[3] The first Mark was written between 30 and 60 and the second about 65. W. L. Knox (1952) has identified nine separate sources

---

[1] *The Gospel according to St. Mark*, pp. 90ff.
[2] *The Sources of the Second Gospel.*
[3] *St. Mark's Gospel: Two Stages of its Making*, p. 1.

which existed as independent units before their incorporation by Mark in his Gospel in its present form.[1] These, together with other written matter used by Mark, would account for almost the whole of the Gospel as we have it.

The difficulty with such views is that they are necessarily speculative and so much depends on subjective considerations. We have no means of identifying or comparing the supposed written sources, as they apparently fell into disuse after their incorporation in Mark's Gospel and ceased to exist as separate entities. We have actually no external evidence that they ever did exist. The theorists are also often opposed to one another in their conclusions about the origin of particular passages.

A general conclusion, which would incorporate what is of value in many of the suggestions here considered, would be that Mark depended on the material circulating in the oral period, that he had the authority of Peter for much of what he wrote, that probably some of Jesus' teaching and quite possibly some narratives were already in written form, although fragmentary,[2] and that no attempt had yet been made to set out in a systematic arrangement an account of Jesus' ministry from its beginning until the end. This study reinforces the pioneer nature of Mark's labours.

THE AUTHORSHIP OF MARK'S GOSPEL

The tradition of the early Church was that the book was written by one called Mark. This dates from the time of Papias and there was never any real doubt

---

[1] *The Sources of the Synoptic Gospels*, vol. i: *St. Mark*, p. 150.
[2] See H. A. Guy: *The Origin of the Gospel of Mark*.

among early Christians. The Mark who is thus named is taken to be the man who is called John Mark in the New Testament—Acts 12: 12, 25; 13: 5, 13; 15: 36–37; Col. 4: 10; 1 Pet. 5: 13; Phil. 24; 2 Tim. 4: 11.

(i) The style of the book, with its rough-and-ready mode of writing and its occasional lapses in grammar and phraseology, suggests one who was not a polished writer in Hellenistic Greek; he knew the language and could write quite forcefully in it, but it was not his native language. John Mark, who was presumably a native of Jerusalem, would have Aramaic as his mother tongue, although no doubt able to speak the common Greek which would be needed on his travels. But he would probably have occasionally to translate his thoughts, naturally expressed in Aramaic, into Greek. This would account for the presence of Aramaisms in the Gospel.

(ii) The writer was vague about the geography of northern Palestine and sometimes made confusing statements or actual mistakes. He often does not state which part of Galilee he is referring to (e.g. 6: 31) and the disciples wander to and from 'the other side' of the Lake in a very confusing way (6: 45; cf. 5: 1, 21). The disciples start from an unnamed place to go to Bethsaida (6: 45), but they arrive at Gennesaret (6: 53), which is quite a different district, and do not arrive at Bethsaida until considerably later (8: 22). In the meantime they have visited Phoenicia (7: 24) and made a journey by a quite incredible route to Decapolis (7: 31). Reference to a map will show that it is impossible to make a coherent account of these travels. The narrative suggests a writer who did not know northern Palestine at all well. John Mark would be more familiar with Judea and the neighbourhood of Jerusalem.

(iii) The book does not suggest the work of an eye-witness, although there are traits that suggest an eye-witness as one authority behind the narrative. The only place where there is a hint of personal presence is in the strange incident at Gethsemane told in 14: 51–52, where it has been suggested Mark himself was the 'young man'.

(iv) The rough character of the book may also be regarded as according with the character of Mark as portrayed in the Acts—probably impulsive and some-what unreliable, but sufficiently attractive to be defended by his cousin Barnabas and later to become reconciled to Paul himself. One would expect this John Mark to write a book such as this, with all its faults and yet its attractiveness and charm.

THE DATE OF MARK'S GOSPEL

If the book was written by John Mark, the date must obviously be in the apostolic era. The evidence of early Christian writers is not decisive in seeking to fix it more exactly. An early Prologue to the Gospel says that it was written after the death of Peter. This is agreed by Irenaeus (about 185), who says that he wrote after the deaths of Peter and Paul—that he 'transmitted in writing the things preached by Peter'. Clement of Alexandria (about 200), however, says that he wrote while Peter was still preaching in Rome. Later tradition spoke sometimes as if he almost wrote at the dictation of Peter, but the general consensus agreed with the words of Papias, that Mark simply put down Peter's preaching without specifying when.

The date usually accepted now for the writing of the Gospel is between 65 and 70, for the following reasons:

(i) Peter and Paul were probably both put to death in the persecution under Nero, in 64–65. The death of his master was probably one of the reasons which impelled John Mark to take this work in hand.

(ii) There is a warning in the apocalyptic passage, 13: 14, of 'the abomination of desolation standing where he ought not'. (The phrase is literally 'the appalling horror' or 'profanation' and is quoted from Daniel and 1 Maccabees, where it refers to a heathen altar set up in the Temple court by Antiochus Epiphanes in 168 B.C.) The reference in Mark seems to be studiously vague, as if the writer were not sure what form the 'abomination' would take. A strange point of grammar is that he uses a masculine participle for 'standing', whereas the Greek word for 'abomination' is neuter. This suggests that he thought the climax of the apocalyptic 'signs' (all of which were to happen in that generation) would be the appearance of a personal evil force, such as the Jews spoke of under the name of Anti-Messiah or Anti-Christ. We know that this did not come about; but in 70 the Roman armies, after the capture of Jerusalem, entered the Temple courts and set the buildings on fire. If Mark had been writing after the fall of Jerusalem, he would surely, thinking of the Roman standards in the Temple, have altered the participle to the usual neuter and would have been more definite—'the abomination of desolation set up in the Temple', or some such phrase. This is what Matthew does (24: 15), writing later, while Luke boldly changes Mark's phrase to 'Jerusalem encompassed by armies' (21: 20). The vague phrases in

Mark suggest that the final siege had not yet begun, but he feared the worst yet dared not be more definite about the horrors to come.

(iii) A note of persecution and suffering runs through many parts of the Gospel. Jesus warns his disciples about the need for taking up a cross (8: 34); the disciples must drink his own cup (10: 38f) and must learn to serve and suffer, following the example of the Son of Man (10: 45). They must learn not to be ashamed of him and his words (8: 38) and are promised ample compensation (10: 29f). The emphasis in such passages would be of special comfort to the Christians who were living in the shadow of persecution in the time of Nero.

(iv) A date towards the end of the first generation of Christians is most likely in view of the needs of the Church of that time. The reasons given in chapter II which led to the writing of a Gospel are particularly applicable to such a time.

The place of writing is generally taken to be Rome, although other places, such as Antioch and Alexandria, have been suggested. It is certain that Mark wrote for Gentile readers. When he quotes Aramaic words of Jesus, he translates them for the benefit of his readers (5: 41; 7: 11, 34; 15: 22) and goes out of his way to explain the Jewish practice of ritual-washing (7: 3-4). There are also a number of Latin words (in their Greek form)—such as legion (5: 9), denarius (12: 15), quadrans (12: 42), praetorium (15: 16) and centurion (15: 39)—but this is not decisive for Rome as the place of writing, as these words were regularly used in Hellenistic Greek. Early writers (Clement, Irenaeus) say the Gospel was written at Rome.

THE CONCLUSION OF THE GOSPEL

In the Revised Version there is a space after the last words of Mark 16: 8—'for they were afraid'—and the margin indicates the doubt about the rest of the chapter. The evidence is overwhelming that the writing of Mark ends with these words:

(i) The oldest texts finish at this point. These include the Greek manuscripts, the Sinai and the Vatican codices, and the most trustworthy copies in Latin, Syriac, Armenian and Georgian versions. The copies used by Matthew and Luke also finished here.

(ii) In the majority of manuscripts verses 9–20 are given after verse 8. But early Church writers up to the end of the fourth century used Greek copies which did not contain this passage and most of those which do are late. The warning given in chapter I must be heeded here—that MSS. must not simply be counted; their value and evidence must be weighed. The weight of the evidence is against the inclusion of verses 9–20 as part of Mark's Gospel.

(iii) This conclusion is borne out by an examination of the contents of the passage. It is a summary of resurrection appearances, but it appears to be based on the accounts in other books. Luke's story of the walk to Emmaus and the appearance of Jesus in Jerusalem are referred to in verses 12 and 14–15, while verses 17–18 seem to reflect the adventures of disciples in the Acts; the reference to Mary Magdalene in verse 9 seems to come from John. As all these books were written later than Mark, this paragraph could not have been composed by that author.

(iv) Examination of the style and vocabulary bears out this conclusion. Both are quite un-Markan. One

can sense even in an English translation how the
graphic style of Mark is suddenly dropped at verse 8
and a smoother style is adopted, beginning with a
reference to Mary Magdalene as if she has not been
already mentioned.

This passage is evidently an early attempt to supply
a suitable conclusion to the Gospel. An Armenian MS.
written in the tenth century has a note above it—'of
the presbyter Ariston'—but this is probably a late
guess by a scribe. We do not know who wrote verses
9–20.

(v) Another attempt was made to conclude the
Gospel, which is found in some MSS. and versions
—with or without verses 9–20. (These are called
respectively the Shorter and the Longer Conclusions.)
This short passage is printed in Moffatt's translation
of the New Testament.

We are thus faced with a problem: How did Mark's
Gospel originally end? Why was it thought necessary
to supply these later 'Conclusions'? The problem is
accentuated by the fact that, in the Greek, verse 8
finishes with a conjunction (*gar*—the Greek word for
'for'). This word could be used to end a sentence or
even a paragraph (as it does sometimes in the Greek
version of the Old Testament), but would seem to be a
very abrupt ending of a book. There are two possible
answers:

Some scholars think that Mark did finish his
Gospel here, with the women running from the tomb
in fear and keeping silence about what they had seen
and heard. It is held that such an ending is thoroughly
Markan. The message of the Gospel ends, as it
began (1 : 22–27), on a note of astonishment and awe.
There was no need for Mark to tell of resurrection

G

appearances of Jesus, for these were well known. The climax of the 'good news' is the proclamation: 'He is risen' (16: 6).

Other scholars insist that a Gospel could not have ended on such an unsatisfactory note. Earlier in the book the writer has hinted at an appearance in Galilee (14: 28; 16: 7) and he would not cease his work until he had recounted this. Streeter suggests that the lost ending of Mark was the document which lay behind the story of the incident in Galilee told in John 21.

These are hence a number of possibilities of what happened to the rest of Mark's account:

(i) The writer may have been interrupted before he could set down anything further. Perhaps he intended to revise and complete his work but could not. He may have died. Such an occurrence has not been unknown in the history of literature; Charles Dickens left the MS. of *Edwin Drood* on his desk one night but died in his sleep, leaving the book unfinished.

(ii) Some think that the conclusion of the book, written by Mark and telling of Jesus' appearance in Galilee, was deliberately suppressed because it conflicted with accounts in Luke and John of appearances in Jerusalem and its neighbourhood. But Matthew's Gospel tells of an appearance in Galilee and the ending of that book was never suppressed.

(iii) The conclusion may have been accidentally lost. If the early form of the Gospel was a papyrus roll, the end of the long sheet would get worn through constant reference and might easily fall off. If the original was a codex, the last page or so might become detached. Streeter suggests that an early copy, if not the very original, was torn in some riot against the Christians in Rome.

Whether the words at 16: 8 were those originally penned by Mark as the conclusion of his book or not, the abrupt conclusion is in keeping with the abrupt opening of the Gospel and the rugged and dramatic nature of this first written proclamation of the Gospel.

CHAPTER IX

THE GOSPEL OF MATTHEW

THE CONSTRUCTION OF MATTHEW'S GOSPEL

The basis of the narrative and the general order of events in this Gospel are Mark's account. As we have seen in chapter IV, the writer has produced what has been called a revised edition of Mark. After his introductory stories in chapters 1 and 2, he follows the Markan order, without deviation, to the end of chapter 4. Chapters 5–7 consist of teaching material from other sources. Then he resumes the Markan narrative (Matt. 8–12), with some variations in the places of events. (See above, p. 42.) From chapter 14 onwards the Markan story is followed, with no variation.

Into this Markan framework the writer has inserted material from other sources. He adds to the narrative, quoting the Old Testament and inserting additional information. This M matter has been discussed in chapter VI. The main departure from Mark is his insertion of blocks of Jesus' teaching. There are five such discourses: the Sermon on the Mount (chapters 5–7), the charge to the twelve apostles (chapter 10), parables (chapter 13), discussion of the relations between disciples (chapter 18) and apocalyptic teaching and parables of judgment (chapters 24–25). Probably chapter 23, consisting of denunciation of the Pharisees, should be added to this last section, the whole consisting of a long enunciation of judgment on the Jews. Each

discourse concludes with a similar formula, such as
'When Jesus had finished these sayings . . .' (7: 28;
11: 1; 13: 53; 19: 1; 26: 1).

Each of these discourses has been compiled by the
writer's method of conflation; he puts together matter
from different sources to form an ordered section of
teaching on a particular topic. Thus the Sermon on the
Mount is composed of Q matter (also in Luke 6: 20-49,
where Jesus delivers the teaching from a 'level place'
—the Sermon on the Plain), other matter taken from
Q (found also in Luke 12: 22ff and other places in
Luke) and considerable matter from the source M.
The charge to the twelve in chapter 10 is based on
Mark 6: 7ff conflated with a similar charge in Q
(found in Luke 10: 1ff), with sayings taken from
Mark 13, Mark 9, M material and Q (cf., for example,
Luke 13: 49-53). The chapter of parables (13) has
as its basis Mark 4, to which the writer has added
parables taken from Q (the mustard seed, although
here conflated with the Markan version, and the
leaven) and his own special source (the tares, the drag-
net, the treasure and the pearl merchant). The
apocalyptic chapter 24 is based on Mark 13, with
matter inserted from a similar apocalypse found in Q
(Luke 17: 22-37).

Matthew's practice of conflating his material makes
it far more difficult to disentangle his sources than is the
case with Luke.

THE CHARACTERISTICS OF MATTHEW'S GOSPEL

From the book itself we can conclude the chief
interests of the writer and see what aspects of the life of
Jesus he wished to enforce.

(i) There is an interest in Judaism and the Jews. This shows itself in four main ways:

(a) There is frequent reference to and quotation from the Old Testament. The writer employs a formula such as 'Then was fulfilled that which was spoken by the prophet . . .' or he says that something happened 'in order that it might be fulfilled which was spoken by the prophet . . .' Some of his references are inexact (the 'quotation' in Matthew 2: 23 cannot be traced in the Old Testament at all) and many of them are applied to events which they certainly never fore-saw (the quotation from Amos in 2: 15 is an historical statement about the Exodus from Egypt; the passage in Jeremiah, in Matthew 2: 17–18, referred to the Jews' going into exile in Babylon; the quotation from Isaiah in 1: 23 did not refer to the Messiah). He introduces Old Testament references to account for Jesus' residence at Capernaum (4: 12–16), for his counselling the silence of those whom he cured (12: 15–21) and for his speaking in parables (13: 34–35). His attach-ment to the literal meaning of a passage leads to a ludicrous result in 21: 2–7, where, not appreciating the parallelism of the Hebrew, where the ass is obviously the same as the colt, he makes Jesus send for two animals and ride into Jerusalem upon both of them. In a somewhat similar vein, Jesus is referred to, some-times in quite inappropriate places, as Son of David (12: 23; 15: 22; 21: 9).

(b) Christianity is regarded as the fulfilment of Judaism. In the Sermon on the Mount Jesus five times repeats an old Law, in order to expound the new and deeper meaning which he gives to it (5: 21–48). Jewish religious observances are assumed to be still in force among Jesus' disciples (6: 1–18). The word 'righteousness' is used to describe the Christian life (5: 20; 6: 1). Only in Matthew is this word, which is at the root of Jewish religion, found on the lips of Jesus. (Paul is very fond of it, but in a different sense).

(c) There is an anti-Jewish tone about the book, in spite of this. The writer particularly emphasizes the failure of the Jewish religious leaders. Pharisees and Sadducees are 'lumped together' in an uncritical fashion. John the Baptist denounces them (3: 7; cf. Luke 3: 7, where his words are addressed to 'the people' simply) and they come together to test Jesus by demanding a 'sign' (16: 1; cf. 16: 6). The bitterest tirade against Pharisees and scribes in any first century Christian literature is in Matthew 23, and many critics, both Jewish and Christian, feel that Jesus' attitude was not so extreme as it is here depicted. The parable of the two sons (Matt. 21: 28–32), obviously directed against the Jews, is found only in this Gospel.

(d) The work of Jesus is portrayed as confined to Jews. The twelve disciples are expressly told not to go to Samaria or Gentile countries (10: 5). Although Mark had written that Jesus went to Phoenicia and entered a house and met a Greek woman (7: 24–25), this writer makes her 'come out from those borders' to meet Jesus (15: 22), who declares that he is not intended for such people (15: 24). This limitation, lasts only until the resurrection. In the final paragraph of the Gospel Jesus commissions the disciples to preach to all nations (28: 19).

(ii) There is an interest in eschatology and the apocalyptic elements of Jesus' teaching. References to this in Mark are often heightened. The statement in Mark 9: 1 about the 'coming of the Kingdom with power' is interpreted to mean the coming of the Son of Man (Matt. 16: 28). The question of the disciples about the destruction of the Temple (Mark 13: 4) is altered to refer to Christ's 'coming and the consummation of the age' (Matt. 24: 3). The writer adds to Mark's reference to the appearing of the Son of Man (13: 26–27) conventional apocalyptic 'signs' such as the mourning of the earth's inhabitants and a great trumpet to summon the elect (24: 30–31). Throughout this chapter Matthew relates everything to the Son of Man's 'coming' (the Greek word *parousia*, frequent in Paul, occurs in the Gospels only in Matthew).

This characteristic is especially discernible in the M matter. This includes the parables of the tares and the drag-net, to which eschatological explanations are added which seem to be out of tune with the parables themselves (13: 24–30, 37–40, 47–50), the parable of the maidens at the wedding, with its exhortation to watch (25: 1–13) and of the judgment (or the sheep and the goats) (25: 31–46). Five times Matthew reproduces the conventional apocalyptic phrase, 'There shall be the weeping and gnashing of teeth' (13: 42, 50; 22: 13; 24: 51; 25: 30) and the term 'the consummation of the age' (mistranslated as 'the end of the world') occurs five times (13: 39, 40, 49; 24: 3; 28: 20).

(iii) The miraculous element is heightened. In Mark's story of the fig-tree near Jerusalem, Peter notices on the day following Jesus' words that it has withered (11: 20). Matthew makes it wither 'immediately' after Jesus speaks (21: 19). The madman in the country of the Gerasenes (Mark 5: 1–20) becomes two madmen with demons (Matt. 8: 28ff) and Bartimaeus at Jericho (Mark 10: 46–52) is likewise duplicated (Matt. 20: 29ff); a very similar story of two blind men is told in 9: 27. Miraculous signs are introduced which are absent from the other Gospels—an earthquake and rending of the rocks, the opening of tombs at the crucifixion (27: 51–53) and a 'great earthquake' and the descent of an angel to roll away the stone of the tomb at the resurrection (28: 2–4).

(iv) There is a strong ecclesiastical interest. The word 'church' occurs in the Gospels only in Matthew —in words to Peter at Caesarea Philippi (16: 18) and in teaching on the settling of disputes (18: 17). In a number of places the writer seems to have in mind the conception of a Christian community. The book was probably written so that, among other uses, it could be employed as a manual of instruction for people who were being received into the Church; its arrangement of Jesus' teaching would facilitate easy reference. It has been suggested that the writer's intention was to supplement Mark, so that a book would be available which would be adequate for public reading in the services of the Church.[1]

The Authorship of Matthew's Gospel

From the book itself we should never conclude that it was the work of one of the original apostles of Jesus. Our study has brought out these points:

(i) The basis of the book is not the reminiscences of an eye-witness or apostle but is Mark's Gospel, which was itself written by one who was not an apostle.

(ii) The treatment of Mark's Gospel shows that the writer is one stage further removed from eye-witnesses. He alters Mark's narrative in ways which make the account less vivid and realistic, considerably abbreviating the miracle-stories and reproducing the words of

[1] G. D. Kilpatrick: *The Origins of the Gospel according to St. Matthew.*

Jesus or his disciples which show the influence of later reflection (see above, pp. 44–46). His account is sometimes confused because of a misunderstanding of Mark's words: Mark describes two occasions in 16: 1–2—the women bought spices after the end of the Sabbath (on Saturday after 6 p.m.) and went to the tomb early Sunday morning; Matthew mixes the two and so produces an impossible note of time (28: 1).

(iii) The author is out of touch with the historical and religious situation in Palestine in the time of Jesus. He makes a Greek woman (whom he calls, by perhaps a deliberate anachronism, a Canaanite) address Jesus as Son of David, a Jewish Messianic title (15: 21). He puts together Pharisees and Sadducees, in spite of their great differences and mutual enmity (3: 7; 16: 1, 6).

(iv) The additions and alterations made to the Markan narrative are improbable in themselves. It is not likely that the crowd thought that Jesus was the Messiah at an early stage in the ministry (12: 23). It is more likely that James and John came to Jesus demanding the chief places than that their mother asked for them, as Matthew says, and that Jesus entered Jerusalem sitting on one animal and not on two. Matthew says that Jesus healed the blind and the lame in the Temple court at Jerusalem (21: 14) but it is more probable that his last act of healing was that performed on Bartimaeus at Jericho, as Mark reports; the situation in Jerusalem was quite different. All these instances betray the hand of a later writer, not an eyewitness.

(v) The narratives which are peculiar to this Gospel constitute the least trustworthy of all the strata which go to the making of the Synoptics. The birth-stories (1–2) conflict with Luke's account of the circumstances of Jesus' infancy. The additions to the Passion story are doubtful—the dream of Pilate's wife, his washing of his hands, the manner of Judas' death, the sealing and guarding of the tomb—while the accounts of the earthquake and resurrection of the saints at the crucifixion and the descent of the angel at the resurrection border on the stories which are found in the apocryphal Gospels, where the tendency is always to heighten the marvellous with such details.

All we would conclude from the Gospel itself is that the writer was a Jewish Christian. He had often been compared to the scribe who is mentioned in Matthew 13: 52. He sought to present Jesus to the Jews as the Messiah and Son of David, making use of 'things old and new'. He wrote probably for Jewish Christians, seeking to show how the events were 'fulfilments' of Old Testament prophecies; he thought of Christianity as a new Law and the Christian Church as the new Israel. In this way he showed that Judaism had been superseded.

THE WORDS OF PAPIAS ABOUT MATTHEW

In early Christian tradition the book was ascribed to Matthew the apostle. This opinion was probably derived from some words of Papias. In addition to his statement about Mark, he reports the Elder as saying: 'Matthew arranged (or composed) the oracles (Greek: *logia*) in the Hebrew language and each one interpreted them as he was able'.

Almost every word in this short sentence requires investigation. (a) In the second word the Greek MSS. differ. Some have 'arranged' or 'put in order' (*synetaxato*), while others have 'wrote' or 'composed' (*synegrapsato*). (b) 'Hebrew' without doubt means Aramaic—the popular language of Palestine, a Syriac dialect which was written in Hebrew characters. The classical Hebrew in which the Old Testament was written was not used among Jews then except in the Scripture readings in the synagogues and a popular translation had to be made into Aramaic in Palestine and into Greek in foreign countries. (c) The word *logia* means 'oracles' or 'sayings'—not quite the same as the usual word for 'sayings' or 'words', which was *logoi* (plural of *logos*). (d) The word 'interpreted' may mean 'translated' or may indicate application or interpretation or explanation.

Regarding the meaning of Papias' words, there are four possibilities:

(i) He may have meant our Gospel of Matthew. This was evidently the view among early Christian writers. It is possible that the Elder (if the reading 'arranged'—*synetaxato*—is the right one) was contrasting Matthew's Gospel, with its orderly arrangement of Jesus' teaching, with Mark's, which he criticised on account of its lack of 'order' (*taxis*).

If Papias did mean our Gospel of Matthew, it is clear that he made a mistake, both in attributing it to the apostle and in thinking it was written in Aramaic. Our Gospel does not show any signs of being a translation from Aramaic. It was written in Greek and at least one of the sources used by the writer—the Gospel of Mark—was a Greek work which we still possess. The other main source—the document Q—was probably also in Greek. We can only hazard a guess why Papias should have attributed the Gospel to the apostle Matthew. Perhaps it was because he noticed that Levi the tax-collector (Mark 2: 14) is called Matthew here (Matt.

9: 9); the title of tax-collector is also given to Matthew in the list of apostles (Matt. 10: 3; cf. Mark 3: 18). It was evidently assumed that Matthew was the same as Levi, by the writer of this Gospel (although this is not at all certain), and so the name of Matthew became attached to it, probably as a consequence of Papias' words.

(ii) Papias may have been referring to an Aramaic Gospel, which is now lost. We know that there was a Gospel of the Hebrews and a Gospel according to the Nazarenes. Papias speaks of a number of attempts to translate the *logia:* perhaps he thought that the Greek 'Matthew' was one translation of one of these Aramaic books.

The alternative to these two views is that he did not mean a Gospel, but one of the sources of our Gospels:

(iii) He may have meant a collection of Old Testament texts. Paul uses the word *logia* when speaking of his Bible—'The oracles of God'. There is evidence that the first Christian written works were collections of passages, which have been called books of 'Testimonies'; they demonstrated ways in which, so the Christians thought, the Old Testament prophets and other writers bore testimony to the coming of Jesus. The apostle Matthew may have compiled such a collection (although one would hardly expect a former tax-collector, if he were one, to be interested in this). Papias' phrase, 'each one interpreted them as he was able' might then mean that each Christian preacher or teacher applied the Old Testament texts as he thought suitable. Our Gospel of Matthew may have been one such attempt, for it is characterised by constant reference to the Old Testament.

(iv) The *logia* may have been a collection of sayings of Jesus. Streeter thought that it consisted of 'prophetic oracles' uttered by Jesus. Many have assumed that it was the document Q. It may have been the sayings which we call M, for these are often Judaistic in tone. Both the Q and M material were probably originally in Aramaic. On this view, the 'oracles' of Jesus were arranged or written down by Matthew, first in Aramaic. This is contrasted by Papias with the Gospel of Mark, which was not written 'in order' and did not make any attempts to 'give a connected account of the Lord's oracles'.

Against this view, however, is the fact that the sayings of Jesus were known among the early Christians as *logoi*, not *logia*.

In the case of the last two interpretations of Papias' words, the name of Matthew would have become attached to the Gospel because the writer used the *logia* compiled by Matthew, as a source.

We have to conclude that at present we do not know for certain what Papias meant. Many scholars incline today to the view that he did mean our Greek Gospel, but made a mistake both in thinking that it was originally written in Aramaic and in considering it was the work of Matthew. They point out that Papias is not a very reliable authority; Eusebius himself, who reports his words, says elsewhere that he was 'a man of small intelligence'. The tendency in some quarters at least is to discount his testimony and to consider it as merely a curiosity of early tradition.

THE DATE OF MATTHEW'S GOSPEL

The following considerations help to a conclusion about this:

(i) It is obviously later than Mark, which we may fairly certainly date between A.D. 65 and 70.

(ii) The language used in 22: 6–7 (an intrusion into the parable of the marriage feast) suggests that the writer knew of an occasion when a ruler did destroy those who ill-treated his servants and 'burned their city'—the destruction of Jerusalem by the Romans in A.D. 70 would immediately come to the mind of a Jew. The addition of the word 'desolate' in 23: 38 (cf. Luke 13: 35, where the word does not occur in the Greek) points in the same direction—that the writer knew of the desolation of Jerusalem and the Temple. So does his alteration of Mark's vague phrase, 'the abomination of desolation standing where he ought not' (Mark 13: 14), to 'standing in the holy place' (Matt. 24: 15).

(iii) A date considerably after the actual events is suggested by the phrase 'to this day' (paralleled in Old Testament accounts written a good time after the events)—in the naming of the 'field of blood' (17: 8) and the story about the stealing of the body of Jesus (28: 15). The lack of distinction between Jewish parties, already noted (3: 7; 16: 1, 6) suggests that it was no longer valid when he wrote. The Sadducees as a party ceased to exist with the destruction of the Temple in 70.

(iv) There are suggestions in the book that the hope of the Parousia (the return of Christ) had grown dim and the author sought to revive it. He assured his readers that the Son of Man would come before the missionaries had finished their work (10: 23). He adds the word 'immediately' to the Markan source in 24: 29, intending to tell his readers that the 'signs' were imminent.

(v) The teaching about the treatment of erring brethren (18: 15–17) suggests the discipline of an ordered Christian community and the way in which 'false prophets' are referred to (7: 15ff) suggests dangers within the Church which were to be found towards the end of the first century (cf. 1 John, 4: 1ff; 2 John, verse 10). The instruction to the disciples to administer baptism in the name of the Trinity (28: 19) is also indicative of a late date, for the evidence in the Acts shows that the early practice was to baptize converts 'in the name of Jesus' (Acts 2: 38; 10: 48; 19: 5).

(vi) The legendary nature of much of the M narrative (see above, p. 98) also suggests a considerable lapse of time, for such matter to develop.

For these reasons the date usually assigned to Matthew is A.D. 85 or some time later. Various places of writing have been suggested. It was obviously written in a place where Jewish Christians predominated, and so was not produced at any centre in Europe. The most likely place is somewhere in Syria—perhaps Antioch—or further east, in northern Assyria.

CHAPTER X

THE GOSPEL OF LUKE

THE CONSTRUCTION OF LUKE'S GOSPEL

As with Matthew, the general order in Luke follows the Markan outline. In no major instance does the writer alter the sequence of events in Mark. He differs from Matthew in that he omits considerable sections of Mark; the chief is Mark 6: 45 to 8: 26 and the smaller sections are 6: 19–29; 10: 1–10; 11: 12–14, 20–25. All of these have been discussed above (pp. 48ff).

Luke's material consists of Q and L, in addition to Mark. He does not conflate his sources, as Matthew does, but gives blocks of Markan and non-Markan matter. It is thus easier, if the scheme of different colours has been used, to see by a glance at the New Testament what source Luke is following in any passage. Where matter overlaps, he sometimes omits one account. He gives his L account of Jesus' visit to Nazareth (4: 16–30) instead of Mark's (6: 1–6) and Q's account of the parable of the mustard seed (Luke 13: 18–19) and the charge about Beelzebub (11: 14ff), in preference to Mark's. But he occasionally reproduces similar matter from two sources. Thus he gives two accounts of the charge to the disciples—from Mark 6: 7–13 in 9: 1ff and from Q in 10: 1ff—and two apocalypses—from Mark 13 in 21: 5ff and from Q in 17: 20ff.

The Gospel is accordingly built on this plan:

Chapters 1–2: Birth-stories of John and Jesus (L).
   3: 1 to 4: 30—from Q and L.
   4: 31 to 6: 11—from Mark 1: 21 to 3: 6.
   6: 12 to 8: 4—from Q and L.
   8: 5 to 9: 50—from Mark 4–6 and 8–9.
   9: 51 to 18: 14—from Q and L.
   18: 15–35—from Mark 10.
   19: 1–28—from L.
   19: 29 to 22: 13—from Mark 11–13.
   22: 14 to 24: 53—from L, with matter from Mark
    14–16.

LUKE'S METHOD OF CONSTRUCTION

This outline makes it plain that there are consider-able sections of Luke which have no Markan matter in them. What procedure did Luke adopt, in thus alternating Markan and non-Markan matter? There are two views about this:

(a) That Luke based his Gospel on Mark, as did the writer of Matthew, and introduced into the Markan outline the material taken from Q and L. He did this in an orderly fashion, keeping the sections separate. In two big sections (6: 12 to 8: 4 and 9: 51 to 18: 14) he abandoned his Markan outline, to return to it after he had incorporated this Q and L matter. These passages have consequently been called the Lesser and the Greater Interpolations respectively, for they are considered as non-Markan interruptions of the Markan account. In the story of the Passion and trial of Jesus he also followed the Markan outline but introduced several distinctive features from L, which was here either a separate written source or consisted of oral material.

(b) That Luke first combined the Q and L material and added Markan passages later. In this case the basis of his Gospel is not Mark but the non-Markan sections. It is held that there was a 'First Draft' of the Gospel, before the writing of the book as we have it now, which did not contain any Markan matter. This theory of its composition is called the Proto-Luke hypothesis and was first put forward by Streeter in 1921, was fully expounded by him in *The Four Gospels* (1924) and developed by Vincent Taylor in *Behind the Third Gospel* (1926).

Proto-Luke consists of the following passages: 3: 1 to 4: 30; 6: 12 to 8: 4; 9: 51 to 18: 14; 19: 1–28; 22: 14 to 24: 53. The birth-stories (chapters 1–2) are not included, as it is thought that these were added to the completed Gospel; the dedication to Theophilus (1: 1–4) was added last of all, before publication.

The main arguments for this theory are as follows:

(i) Luke begins his Gospel, not with Markan matter, but with material from L and Q (3: 1ff). This opening, with its elaborate dating, reads indeed like the beginning of a book. The end of the Gospel similarly consists of his own distinctive matter (24: 13–53). This suggests that the author thought of his non-Markan matter as the framework of his book, into which he inserted Markan matter.

(ii) The QL sections read like a complete book—a Gospel in itself. There are here most of the essential parts of the story—John the Baptist's preaching, the baptism of Jesus and the temptations, his teaching at Capernaum and Nazareth, his healing, his treatment of sinners and outcasts, the journey to Jerusalem, the treatment of Samaritans and would-be followers, the sending out of the disciples to preach, teaching about prayer and riches and eschatology; and the trial of Jesus and his appearances after the resurrection. On the other hand, the Markan passages in Luke do not read like a connected story; they are interpolated into the non-Markan framework.

(iii) Where there are parallel narratives in the two sources—Mark and Q or L—Luke prefers the non-Markan. Thus he gives the accusation of Jesus' enemies that he was using the power of Beelzebub, from Q (Luke 11: 14-22), ignoring the Markan account (Mark 3: 22-30). Quite early in his Gospel he gives the story of Jesus' rejection at Nazareth (4: 16-30), so he does not reproduce the account from Mark 6: 1-6 when he reaches that point in the Markan narrative. In 7: 36-50 he gives the story of Jesus' being anointed by a woman in Galilee; so when he comes to the Markan account of an anointing at Bethany (Mark 14: 3-9), he omits it. In reproducing chapter 1 of Mark he leaves out one small paragraph, about the call of the first disciples (Mark 1: 16-20), but substitutes his account of the call of Peter (Luke 5: 1-11). He omits the request of James and John, with Jesus' teaching about service (Mark 10: 35-45), for he gives similar teaching in Jesus' words at the Last Supper (Luke 22: 24-27). It will be noted that in some cases his use of Q or L parallel matter comes before he reaches a point in the Markan outline and sometimes it comes later in his Gospel; but in each case he rejects the Markan story and keeps the non-Markan. These facts suggest that he had already written this before he came across or incorporated Markan matter.

(iv) This view explains why the Markan matter is in solid 'blocks'. It suggests that this was a later addition to a book already written or at least drafted. Luke's treatment is in marked contrast to Matthew's, where the writer evidently had both Mark and Q before him and used them simultaneously, conflating both with his special traditions (M).

Streeter suggested that Proto-Luke was composed while Luke was staying at Caesarea with Paul. The record shows an interest in the Herod family and in Samaritans, and Caesarea was a port through which Galilaeans and Samaritans both passed. If this theory is correct, it means that we have another valuable early witness to the Gospel story, alongside of Mark, written possibly before this first of our Gospels.

This theory has not received unanimous support from New Testament scholars and there are those who hold that Luke used Mark as the basis of his book or put together Markan and non-Markan matter alternately as he wrote. They think that the QL material does not form a complete story and would be inadequate as the presentation of the Gospel; there are certainly big gaps in it. It contained, for instance, no account of the conflict between Jesus and the authorities in Jerusalem. The weakest part of the argument is indeed that relating to the L passion story (Luke 22: 14 to 23: 56). Vincent Taylor answers that there were considerable Markan 'interpolations' made in Proto-Luke, before he issued the final Gospel. But if these later Markan additions are removed, there seems little of a connected account left; the Markan passages, though small in size, seem to act like the mortar which holds the bricks together and without this the structure collapses. And in many places in the later chapters,

Mark seems to be the basis—in the story of Gethsemane (Luke 22: 39–53), Peter's denial (22: 54–62), the crucifixion (23: 33–38), the death and burial (23: 44–56) and the empty tomb (24: 1–12).

Is it possible that Proto-Luke should be considered to extend only to 19: 28 and that for the rest of his book Luke conflated Mark 14–16 with traditions and matter from L?

THE INTERESTS OF LUKE

The author of this Gospel was a Gentile, if the traditional ascription is to be accepted; and apart from this, his writing seems to show it. His book is the most literary of the four and indeed of any New Testament writing. He shows by his opening words that he can write in good classical Greek, for the dedication (4: 1–4) is as impressive in the Greek as in the English version; and he can suddenly change to a swift narrative in a style which recalls the Greek LXX (1: 5 to 2: 39). Some of his peculiar matter is written in fine style in Hellenistic Greek—the Prodigal Son (15: 11–32) and the walk to Emmaus (24: 13–35)—and some of his sentences have a dramatic quality which is equal to the best in contemporary Latin and Greek authors (e.g. 23: 25).

The author was especially concerned to show the origin of Christianity and to trace its progress throughout the Roman world. He had in mind readers like the Theophilus to whom he dedicated his two books (Luke 1–4; Acts 1: 1); there is no doubt that the same man penned both works. His writings have been called 'the first Christian apology'; this was the name given to writings which appeared later, addressed to Roman

officials or even to the Emperor, to defend Christianity
against its enemies and to show that it was not hostile
to the State or dangerous to society. Thus we find in
the Gospel:

(i) The elements in Jesus' actions and teaching which
suggest a wider outlook than a merely Jewish one are
emphasised. Luke records the healing of the centurion's
servant (from Q) and also the healing and the gratitude
of the Samaritan leper (from L). The teaching in the
parables of the Prodigal Son and the Good Samaritan
would appeal to Gentile readers. One cannot imagine
the author of Matthew's Gospel would have included
the last named parable.

(ii) Romans are presented here as favourable to
Jesus, or at least as not hostile. Luke says that three
times Pilate attempted to release Jesus, having acquitted
him (23: 4, 14, 20, 22) and the blame for the crucifixion
is put on the Jews (23: 25; 24: 20). There is the
same note in the Acts, where stress is laid on
the neutral attitude of Roman officials like Gallio
(Acts 18: 12ff).

(iii) The story is put in a world-setting. Reference
is made to the reigning Emperor at the time of Jesus'
birth (2: 1) and the beginning of John's (and presumably Jesus') preaching (3: 1).

LUKE'S PORTRAIT OF JESUS

These aspects of the life and teaching of Jesus are
found this Gospel:

(i) His attitude towards the poor and outcast. Jesus
blesses the poor (6: 20–21; cf. Matt. 5: 3, 6). In three
parables the dangers of wealth are pointed out (12:

14ff; 16: 1ff, 19ff). Jesus befriends a sinful woman
(7: 37ff), a crucified criminal (23: 39–43), tax-collectors and sinners (15: 1ff; 19: 1–10).

(ii) Women are mentioned with special tenderness
and interest. Mary and Elizabeth are the central
figures in the first two chapters. Jesus has sympathy
for a widow (7: 12) and for both Mary and Martha
(10: 38–42) and the weeping women of Jerusalem
(23: 27ff). Not only men but women figure in the
Lukan parables (15: 3–7, 8–10).

(iii) Samaritans and Gentiles are treated differently
from the other Gospels. From the beginning Jesus'
mission cannot be confined to the Jews (4: 24ff). He
refuses to avenge himself on a Samaritan village
(9: 52–56) and makes one of that despised race
the hero of a parable (10: 30–35) and an incident
(17: 12ff).

(iv) Luke mentions the Spirit of God more than any
other evangelist. This is central in the birth stories
(1: 15, 35, 67; 2: 25–26). Jesus is guided by the Spirit
(4: 1, 14, 18; 10: 21) and the highest gift to men from
God is his Spirit (11: 13; cf. Matt. 7: 11, which probably represents the wording in Q).

(v) Prayer is prominent in Luke's Gospel. He gives
instances of Jesus' praying—at his baptism (3: 21),
before choosing the disciples (6: 12), at Caesarea
Philippi (9: 18), before teaching about prayer (11: 1ff)
and on the cross (23: 34, 46). Three parables about
prayer are found only in Luke (11: 5–9; 18: 1–8, 9–14).
Hymns of praise are found at the beginning of the
story (1: 46ff, 67ff; 2: 14, 29ff) and the book ends on
the same note (24: 52–53).

THE AUTHORSHIP OF THE BOOK

The conclusion drawn from the opening phrases in Luke and the Acts is confirmed by other considerations. The Greek style is the same in both books and there are the same general ideas and 'scheme'. In the Gospel Luke traces the story of Jesus from Galilee to Jerusalem; in the Acts he traces the spread of Christianity from Jerusalem to Rome. The following are the main reasons for attaching the name of Luke to both these books:

(i) Early tradition and testimony is that the author was named Luke. As he was a comparatively obscure member of the Church, it is difficult to imagine their being attributed to him unless he had at least some hand in their composition.

(ii) In the Acts there are three sections, known as the 'we-passages', where the writer uses the first person plural instead of the third person (16: 10–17; 20: 6 to 21: 18; 28: 1–16). The obvious conclusion is that the writer was himself present on these occasions and he seems to be reproducing matter from a diary. Our investigation is thus narrowed to finding among Paul's circle of companions one who was present with him.

(iii) There are phrases in the books which suggest a medical knowledge—'a great fever' (Luke 4: 38), 'full of leprosy' (in the advanced stages) (5: 12), 'his feet and ankle-bones received strength' (Acts 3: 7). The somewhat unkind words of Mark about doctors (5: 26) are modified in Luke (8: 43). . . . Cadbury subjected the language of the two books to a thorough examination and concluded that it is not more technical than might be expected from an educated layman of the first century. This does not, of course, rule out the possibility that the writer was a doctor, but it does not prove he was; the question cannot be decided on the ground of the language alone.

(iv) When we study the names of Paul's companions in the Acts and his own letters, some are naturally excluded—for instance Silas and Timothy, who are mentioned by name in the Acts, the former in a 'we-passage' (16: 19ff). Among those who are left, the most likely is Luke, whom Paul refers to in affectionate terms, as a doctor, in Colossians 4: 14.

It seems therefore that Luke had at least something to do with the writing of these books. There are two possibilities:

(i) Luke, the companion and friend of Paul, wrote all of both books. In the Acts he included extracts from his own diary. He may have gathered some of the material for the Gospel when living at Caesarea during Paul's two years of imprisonment there. There are traits in the Gospel which remind us of Paul's teaching; the apostle's doctrine of justification by faith can be found in the parable of the Prodigal Son, and his declaration that in Christ 'there can be neither Jew nor Greek, bond nor free, male nor female' (Gal. 3: 28) is also echoed in the Gospel.

(ii) Luke wrote only the diary, when he was with Paul on his journeys. Another writer made use of this as a source and incorporated it into his book. He re-wrote it in his own style (retaining only 'we' in some places—for the diary may originally have extended over more than the three passages where this now appears), just as he did with Mark in the Gospel. Those who hold this view stress the differences between the narrative in the Acts and the information given by Paul himself in his letters, and the differences between the portraits of Paul in the two. Hence the author cannot have been the close companion of Paul that the diarist was. It was, of course, this author who also wrote the Gospel. The name of Luke became attached to the two books because he was the diarist.

THE DATE OF COMPOSITION OF LUKE'S GOSPEL

Three dates have been suggested for this:

(i) A very early one. The Acts ends with the imprisonment of Paul at Rome (28: 30–31) and some have felt that Luke would not have ended there if he had known of Paul's execution, which probably happened in A.D. 64–65. Hence the book (and the Gospel also) is to be dated before that. It has been suggested that they were written to 'brief' the counsel for Paul's defence at his trial.

There are great difficulties in the way of such an early date, however. Luke's language in 21: 20, where he interprets the vague reference in Mark 13: 14 as meaning the siege of Jerusalem, shows that he at least knew of the events of A.D. 69. Further, the early date would make Mark about A.D. 60 and we have seen that the probable date for Mark's Gospel itself is 65–70. (See chapter VIII.)

(ii) A very late date. Some think that Luke had read the *Antiquities of the Jews*, by Josephus (which was published about A.D. 96), for the Jewish historian mentions a Lysanias (cf. Luke 3: 1) who was put to death in 34 B.C. In this case Luke is wrong in his reference here. This would, however, ascribe great carelessness to Luke, if he took the name from Josephus' book and inserted it in this unsuitable place. An inscription has been discovered which suggests that a man called Lysanias ruled Abilene in the time of Tiberius.

The other suggested case of dependence on Josephus is Acts 5: 36–37, where Luke mentions Theudas and Judas, in the report of Gamaliel's advice. One difficulty is that he has put the two men in the wrong order— Judas revolted against the Romans in A.D. 6 and Theudas in A.D. 44; another puzzle is that Theudas' date is about ten years after Gamaliel's speech. Josephus mentions Theudas and then the sons of Judas, and it is suggested again that Luke carelessly read Josephus' words. But his reliance on the written account is not proved. Streeter suggested that Luke heard Josephus lecture in Rome, some years before the publication of his book, and remembered the two names from hearing them in this way. In any case, Luke was not directly concerned with Jewish history and it is pardonable if he confused the two men.

(iii) An intermediate date—between 75 and 85. The Gospel is probably later than the siege of Jerusalem (cf. Luke 21: 20), as shown above. It is later than Mark (65–70) and time must be allowed for Mark to have been copied and to have become circulated, so that a copy was available for Luke. The Acts shows that the author probably did not know the contents of Paul's letters; his book was written before these were copied and came into general circulation. The reason why he finished his second book with the arrival of Paul at Rome and not with his trial and execution is that he reached his goal at this point. Paul had arrived at Rome; to have told the story of his fate at the hands of the Romans would have been an anti-climax. He may of course have intended the writing of a third volume.

If the Proto-Luke theory is accepted, the first draft of the Gospel would be earlier—perhaps on the arrival at Rome or between 60 and 64. The final edition of the book, combining Markan matter with Q and L material, would still be about A.D. 80. The Gospel was known to Clement of Rome (writing about 96) and probably to the writer of the Fourth Gospel (95–105), so the date is once again fixed before the last decade of the first century.

CHAPTER XI

THE FOURTH GOSPEL:
(1) JOHN AND THE SYNOPTICS

A distinction has been drawn already between the Synoptic Gospels and the Fourth, by the very name given to the first three. Even a cursory reading cannot fail to show the different presentation of the story found in the book known as 'The Gospel according to St. John'. (It is customary in modern books to refer to this as 'the Fourth Gospel'; but for the sake of convenience it is called here simply 'John'. This is not to be taken to imply that it was written by anyone of that name, any more than the use of 'Matthew' in previous chapters means that that Gospel was written by the apostle.)

The following are the ways in which John differs from the Synoptics:

(i) The actual contents differ greatly. There is no account here of the baptism of Jesus or the temptations; none of the Synoptic works of healing is included. There is a different account of the last Supper and no mention of the agony and prayer in Gethsemane. Quite different stories are told of resurrection appearances. The only matter common to all four Gospels is the account of John the Baptist's expectation of a successor (although told differently here), the clearing of the Temple court, the feeding of the five thousand

and walking across the water and the main outlines
of the Passion story—anointing at Bethany, the entry
into Jerusalem, the trial and crucifixion.

(ii) There are considerable differences in chronology,
both in the general 'scheme' of Jesus' work and in
particular events.

(a) In the Synoptics there are no clear indications
of time, apart from the mention of springtime in
Galilee (the ears of corn, Mark 2: 23ff, and the green
grass, Mark 6: 39) and the fact that the crucifixion
occurred in the spring, at Passover time. We cannot
conclude whether Jesus' ministry lasted just over one
year or a number of years, from such data. In John
three Passovers are mentioned (2: 13; 6: 4; 12: 1); if,
as seems likely, these are different years, the ministry
of Jesus here occupies at least two complete years.
There is also mentioned an unnamed 'feast of the
Jews' (5: 1) and the feast of Tabernacles (7: 2), which
took place in September, and the feast of the Dedication
(10: 22), in December. Even with these statements,
however, it is difficult if not impossible to construct a
definite chronology of Jesus' work and to make it fit
the Synoptic story.

(b) In Mark 1: 14 Jesus is said to have begun his
work after the imprisonment of John the Baptist. This
is contradicted in John 3: 30. This author makes them
work alongside for a time (cf. John 4: 1) and the Baptist
gracefully gives way to Jesus and fades from the scene.
(See also below, under vii.)

(c) The clearing of the Temple court takes place
in the Synoptics in the Passion week (Mark 11: 15–18)
and is indeed one, if not the chief, reason for the opposition and plot of the priestly authorities (Mark 11: 18,
27ff). In John, Jesus clears the court on his first visit

to Jerusalem, before he has begun his work in Galilee (John 2: 13–22). It is as if this writer wishes to present the challenge of Jesus to Judaism from the very commencement of his public work, whereas in the Synoptics Jesus' action is the climax of his criticism of the Jewish system.

(d) The Synoptics state or assume that the Last Supper was the Passover meal (Mark 14: 14; Matt. 26: 18; Luke 22: 11). Jesus was arrested on the Passover night and the celebration was over by the time he was executed on the Friday. John states emphatically that the Supper took place 'before the feast of the Passover' (13: 1). The trial before Pilate took place before the eating of the Passover meal (18: 28) and when Pilate passed sentence it was still 'the preparation of the Passover' (19: 14). All four Gospels agree that Jesus died on a Friday. But the Passover meal was not fixed for a definite day of the week but for a day of the month (Nisan 15). In the Synoptics it fell this year on Thursday, in John on Friday and Jesus died that afternoon. The Synoptics further state that Jesus died at three o'clock in the afternoon (Mark 15: 34), having been on the cross for six hours (Mark 15: 25); John states that Pilate was still judging him at noon (19: 14).

It is true that the Synoptic account is not entirely consistent. Jesus' statement in Luke 22: 15–16 suggests that he expected to die before the Passover. It is unlikely that Jesus would have been arrested on the night of the Passover meal, when the carrying of arms would not be allowed. The priests indeed had sought to arrest Jesus before the feast began (Mark 14: 1–2). Some critics favour the Johannine chronology here and think that the meal with the disciples was a Jewish

family celebration, not the actual Passover. But the
statement of Mark 14: 12ff stands and the fourth
evangelist may have fixed the death of Jesus for the
time when the Passover sheep were being killed in the
Temple courts, before the meal, because he wanted to
show that Jesus was the true Paschal lamb and by his
death superseded the Temple system.

(iii) The place of Jesus' work is different. The
Markan scheme, followed in general lines by Luke and
Matthew, places most of his work in Galilee and the
north. He visits Jerusalem only for the last Passover.
In John he is in the neighbourhood of Jerusalem a
number of times (2: 13; 5: 1; 7: 10; 10: 22; 11: 18ff;
12: 1ff). The scene of most of his work is Judea. The
only Galilaean ministry is in chapter 6. When he visits
Capernaum, it is to stay 'not many days' (2: 12),
before he goes to Jerusalem. There is no visit to
Phoenicia or the territory of Herod Philip.

(iv) Most of the narrative of John is thus peculiar
to this Gospel. Instead of the Synoptic miracles of
healing, there are narrated seven 'signs', as the author
calls them—the turning of water into wine (2: 1–11),
the healing of a nobleman's son (4: 46–54), the healing
of a lame man at Jerusalem (5: 1ff), the feeding of the
people (6: 1ff), the walking on the water (6: 16–21),
the healing of a man born blind (9: 1ff), the raising of
Lazarus from the dead (11: 1ff). Each of these is used
to show the development of 'belief' in Jesus, on the
part of disciples or others, or of opposition from his
enemies. In addition there are accounts of interviews
with people unknown to the Synoptics—Nicodemus
(3: 1ff), a Samaritan woman (4: 1ff)—and controversy
between Jesus and the Jews of Jerusalem (5: 10ff;
7: 14ff; 8: 12ff; 10: 24ff).

(v) The teaching of Jesus is differently presented. There are no parables in this Gospel. Instead, Jesus uses allegory and indulges in long discourses, either in controversy with the Jews or in intimate talk with the disciples. Typical of this teaching are the conversation with Nicodemus (3: 1–21), the discourse about the bread of life (6: 32–58), the allegory of the Good Shepherd (10: 1–18) and the talk with the disciples at the Supper (chaps. 13–16). The style is the same throughout, so that it is often difficult to tell where the narrative ends and the teaching begins; the words of Jesus seem to merge into the comments or meditation of the writer (e.g. 3: 10ff).

The subject of Jesus' teaching is likewise different. In the Synoptics his theme is the Kingdom of God; he describes this in parables and speaks of the relations of men with each other, as members of the Kingdom, and as sons of God. His controversy with the Pharisees is over such points as the observance of the Sabbath and other Jewish laws and he condemns the narrow spirit of the scribes. In John the subject of Jesus' teaching is himself. He argues with the Jews over his own claims and impresses these on his disciples. The term Kingdom of God occurs only once (3: 3, 5); instead, frequent mention is made of 'eternal life' as the present possession of the one who accepts Jesus' teaching and believes in him (3: 36; 5: 24; 17: 3).

(vi) The Messiahship of Jesus is differently presented. In the Synoptics this is not acknowledged by any human being until Peter's confession at Caesarea Philippi (Mark 8: 27ff); the disciples are then told not to reveal it to anybody. Silence had already been enjoined on demented people who recognised Jesus (Mark 1: 25–34). Bartimaeus, at Jericho, is the first

person to call Jesus publicly the Son of David (Mark
10: 47) and the first open claim by Jesus himself is in
reply to the question of the High Priest at his trial
(Mark 14: 62). But in John, Jesus is openly recognised
from the beginning—by Philip (John 1: 45), by
Nathanael (1: 49), even by Samaritans (4: 39) and
later by Peter (6: 68–69). Jesus proclaims himself as
the Messiah (4: 26; 9: 37) and asserts his own claims
in controversy with the Jews in Jerusalem (7: 25–36;
8: 12–19, 31–59).

(vii) The account of John the Baptist and his work
differs in several particulars. In the Synoptics John is
a preacher of repentance, proclaiming a coming
judgment. He practises 'baptism for the remission of
sins'. In the Fourth Gospel there is no record of John's
call for repentance and his preaching is subservient to
his expectation of a successor; he is simply presented as
the forerunner of Jesus. In the Prologue he is called
a 'witness' (1:15) and it is emphasised that he was not
the 'light' (1: 8); he himself claims to be nothing more
than a 'voice' (1: 23). At his baptism, which in the
Synoptics is an experience of Jesus himself, the coming
of the Spirit as a dove is presented as a sign for John
himself (1: 32–34). He directs his disciples to Jesus,
pointing to him as 'the lamb of God' (1: 29ff, 36).
The keynote of his ministry is: 'He must increase but
I must decrease' (3: 30). In this Gospel John and
Jesus work alongside for a time, although they never
apparently co-operate. The last mention of John is
in 4: 1 (apart from a reference in 5: 36), where Jesus is
said to have had more success than John. There is no
account of his imprisonment, his message to Jesus from
prison or his death. He simply fades from the scene
when Jesus arrives.

THE RELATION OF THE FOURTH GOSPEL TO THE SYNOPTICS

Some of these distinctions are differences of emphasis but some of them are contradictions of the Synoptic account. They inevitably raise the question: What was the purpose of the writer and what was his relation to the Synoptists? Three suggestions have been made:

(i) That he intended to supplement the Synoptic story, by supplying information which was lacking there—about Jesus' activities in Judea or about his miracles and teaching to the disciples. But in this case, we must ask: Why does his material overlap in some places with the Synoptic matter? Why did he make use of Synoptic material at all, as he certainly seems to have done in some places?

(ii) That he wished to correct the Synoptic story— in matters of chronology, for instance, or in the nature of Jesus' teaching. But in this case we should expect more common matter, if the writer wished to clear up difficulties which he found in them. In some places, indeed, where he disagrees with the Synoptic chronology (e.g. in the dating of the cleansing of the Temple court), his presentation is probably less historical than the Synoptic one. In other cases (e.g. in the dating of the Last Supper and the trial), his chronology is preferred by many modern scholars as being the more likely. His 'correction' of the Synoptic picture of Jesus is not necessarily a true one, for we not only miss the teacher of the Synoptics but the humility of Jesus is replaced by self-assertion and there is little of the compassion which characterised Jesus' attitude towards the crowds (Mark 6: 34).

(iii) That he wished to reinterpret the Synoptic story. (This might embrace also the idea of 'correcting' it.) The Synoptic outline would be familiar to his readers. The writer probably read and used Mark and Luke, although some scholars think that he did not know the written Gospels but was acquainted with the stories which still circulated orally in his neighbourhood. He seems, however, to base the story of the feeding of the people (John 6: 1ff) on Mark 6: 35ff, with Mark 8: 1ff probably also taken into consideration. He uses the Markan story of an anointing at Bethany (Mark 14: 3–9) as the basis of his narrative in 12: 1–8, but he includes details from Luke's story of an anointing in Galilee (Luke 7: 36ff).

Looking at this material from his own distinctive point of view (which we shall consider later), he gave a new presentation to the story. Some think that the healing of the nobleman's son (John 4: 46–54) is the same incident as the healing of the centurion's servant (Luke 7: 2–10; Matt. 8: 5–13), presented as a 'sign' for Galilee. The story of the man at the pool of Bethesda (John 5: 1–18) seems to echo the healing of the paralytic (Mark 2: 1–12); in both accounts the root of the man's trouble seems to be the man's sin and in both he is told to take up his pallet (the same Greek word, not in the best literary phraseology, is used in both) and walk. But in John the story becomes a conflict about the observance of the Sabbath (5: 10ff), like Synoptic narratives (cf. for example, Luke 13: 14). Jesus' answer (5: 17) is reminiscent of Mark 2: 28 and may be John's rewriting of this logion. Then the author uses the narrative to append teaching about the nature of Jesus' authority (5: 19ff). Similarly the story of Nicodemus (3: 1ff) may be the Johannine counterpart of the rich man (Mark 10: 17ff and parallels) and the teaching about being 'born anew' sounds like an echo of the saying in Matthew 18: 3 about becoming like little children, to enter the Kingdom of God. The author seems to be making use of the incident at Caesarea Philippi (Mark 8: 27ff) in Peter's acknowledgment in 6: 66–71. The agony in Gethsemane (Mark 14: 33ff) has its counterpart in Jesus' prayer in John 12: 23ff.

THE OUTLOOK AND THOUGHT OF THE WRITER

The distinctive way in which the story of Jesus is presented throws light upon John's thought and his conception of Christ and Christianity.

(i) The opening words of the Gospel show that he was influenced by Alexandrian Judaism. 'In the beginning was the Word.' The term is the Greek *logos*. The Greek philosopher Heraclitus (about 500 B.C.) had used this to denote the principle of reason within the universe. The world was (to use the word which we derive from this term) 'logical'; it made sense, he thought. The word then became a technical term in Greek philosophy; it was a useful one, because it meant (coming from the verb *legō*, 'I say') not only a word or speech but also reason and discourse. The Jewish philosopher Philo, who lived at Alexandria in the first century (he was born about 20 B.C.) thought he saw in this a way by which Greek philosophy and Hebrew thought could be reconciled. In the Old Testament there are frequent references to the 'word of the Lord'. This came to the prophets; the formula frequently used in their works, 'Thus saith the Lord', is literally 'Word of Yahweh'. According to Gen. 1 the world and universe were made when 'God spoke'. So Philo said that the speech or word of God was the means by which he worked and communicated with men. Philo almost personified the Logos, as an intermediary between God and men.

The opening words of John not only recall Gen. 1: 1 but also link his work at once with the thought of educated people of his time. The Prologue (1: 1–18) is a poem about the Logos; some think that it was composed by another man and existed independently, before being adapted and incorporated in the Gospel.

(ii) He makes, however, a new contribution in verse 14—'the Logos became flesh and dwelt among us'. This was something which neither the Greek philosophers nor Philo had ever conceived. The life of Jesus is hence presented as a manifestation of the incarnate Logos. This is the reason why the picture of Jesus is different from that in the Synoptics. The miracles are 'signs' of his glory, for men who will see. Jesus is self-determined throughout. He is not killed; he 'lays down his life', of his own volition (10: 18). In Gethsemane he is not arrested; he gives himself up (18: 4–8). He does not ask questions, to gain information (as in Mark 5: 30 and 6: 38)—or if, on one occasion, he does, he knows the answer beforehand (John 6: 5–6). He knows, by himself, what is 'in men' and does not need anyone to teach him (2: 24–25). He sees into the characters of people, at a glance—of Peter (1: 42), of Nathanael (1: 47–48), of the Samaritan woman (4: 16–18) and of Judas (6: 70). Emphasis is placed on the power of his words (6: 63), which even his enemies acknowledge (7: 46). All these features of the Johannine Christ are aspects of the divine Logos on earth.

(iii) The revelation of Jesus is described in such terms as 'life', 'light', 'truth' (1: 4–17). Jesus himself claims to be all these (8: 12; 14: 6). The seven 'signs' show his authority over nature, the disciples, disbelievers, the Sabbath, darkness and blindness and death. The climax is the raising of Lazarus. As an historical narrative it has difficulties and it may be regarded not as an actual occurrence but as a dramatisation of Jesus' life-giving power to those who believe in him. It is a 'sermon illustration' on the theme: 'I am the resurrection and the life' (11: 25).

(iv) The greatest reality for the author is the experience of the presence of Christ. He describes this in several ways. In the last discourses with the disciples at supper, Jesus speaks of 'another Comforter'. The Greek word is *Paraclete*, which meant someone 'called in to help' another. It was applied to an advocate in a court of law (hence the R.V. margin—'another advocate'—cf. 1 John 2: 1). In five short passages (14: 15–17, 25–26; 15: 26–27; 16: 5–11, 12–15) the Spirit of God is spoken of as the Paraclete, who will take the place of Jesus when he has gone. The Paraclete will come in answer to the prayer of Jesus, will abide with the disciples and teach them and will bear witness about Jesus.

(v) The eschatology of the writer is distinctive. In this Gospel Jesus speaks of his 'return' (14: 3—the only place in the four Gospels where the phrase, 'I come again', is found), but it is not a coming in power and glory of outward manifestation, but as an eternal presence with the disciples. At times the 'return' of Christ seems to be the same as the coming of the Paraclete. In other places it is possible that the resurrection is intended (14: 19; 16: 16). When, after the resurrection, Jesus does come back to the disciples, he gives them the Spirit (20: 22).

Not only is there no support here for the idea of a future Parousia in power, but the events of the 'last days'—resurrection and judgment—are spoken of as present. Martha's conventional reference to a future resurrection is rebuked (11: 24–26); the judgment of the world is 'now' (12: 31; cf. 3: 18–19). There are some places where the writer seems to adopt the conventional 'futurist' outlook (3: 36; 12: 25; 5: 28–29), but the other emphasis is more prominent and characteristic of the book. Eternal life is here not a blessing reserved for the future but a present reality. The one who believes *has* eternal life (3: 36; 5: 24; 17: 3).

From this study of the actual contents of the book, we can now proceed to see what conclusions can be reached about the circumstances which led to its writing and what we can learn about the author.

CHAPTER XII

THE FOURTH GOSPEL:
(2) AUTHORSHIP AND OTHER PROBLEMS

The question of the authorship of the book has been deliberately left until this point; the book must first be studied, in relation to the Synoptics and by itself, to see what the contents suggest about its author. We can then see more clearly the circumstances of the time and the situation which called forth such a book, and, last of all, endeavour perhaps to assign the book to a definite person, if possible.

THE CIRCUMSTANCES OF WRITING

(i) The narratives in the Synoptic Gospels were generally known in the Church. (See above, pp. 124f.) But it was evidently felt that there was place for a more definitely theological and philosophical presentation. An attempt must be made to set forth the Gospel message in terms of contemporary Jewish and Greek thought. This suggests that the writer had in mind thoughtful and educated people to whom he particularly wished to appeal.

(ii) There were dangers within the Church which he wished to combat. Some Christians deprecated emphasis on the human life of Jesus. Towards the end of the first century some people called Docetists (from

the Greek word *dokeō*, meaning 'seem') said that Jesus
was not really a man and his body was not real flesh
and blood; it only 'seemed' to be. They felt it was
unworthy that the Lord should have been bound by
earthly limitations. This writer, to combat this heresy,
stresses the human side of Jesus' earthly life—his
weariness at the well (4: 6) in Samaria, his human
emotions at the grave of Lazarus (11: 33-35), his
troubled spirit (12: 27; 13: 21) and his thirst on the
cross (19: 28). This is in accordance with his insistence
in the Prologue that the Logos became *flesh*—a man
(1: 14). Some were saying that Jesus had not been
actually crucified, that Simon of Cyrene (Mark 15: 21)
had taken his place; Jesus had escaped from his
'phantom' of a human body and had gone straight to
heaven. So this writer asserts that Jesus carried his
own cross (19: 17) (in spite of the fact that he is con-
tradicting the Synoptics), that he actually died on the
cross (19: 34) and that even after the resurrection his
body bore the marks of his physical wounds (20: 27).

(iii) Some Christians were apparently in danger of
detaching their Christian experience from its roots in
history; theirs was a vague kind of Christianity which
deprecated insistence on the historic life of Jesus of
Nazareth. So this writer holds that the living Christ
of experience is the same as the Jesus of history. In
the Supper discourses he shows that the Christian's
experience of Christ after the resurrection is the same
as that of the disciples with Jesus on earth. He thus
sought to link together in one fellowship those who had
seen and those, his contemporaries, who had not seen
but yet believed (20: 29).

(iv) Some lauded John the Baptist excessively. There
is evidence from the New Testament and other sources

that the followers of John continued as a body for a long time after his death and that his influence was widespread (Acts 18: 24ff; 19: 1ff). Some elevated John above Jesus himself, probably arguing that if it had not been for John's baptism of Jesus and his preparation of the way, Jesus himself would not have undertaken his work. So this writer omits mention of Jesus' baptism, only referring to it incidentally to make it a sign for John (1: 32–34); and throughout he deliberately subordinates John to Jesus. (See above, p. 123.)

(v) Jewish opponents of the Church were active. After the fall of Jerusalem in A.D. 70 the Jewish parties as such largely disappeared. In this Gospel there is no mention of Sadducees and little of Pharisees; Jesus' opponents are generally spoken of simply as 'the Jews'. They misunderstand him from the very beginning (2: 18–20); they complain of his actions and persecute him (5: 10, 15–16; 9: 18) in Jerusalem and even in Galilee they seek to kill him (6: 41, 52; 7: 1, 13) and they argue fiercely about him and his claims (7: 15; 10: 19–24). There is no room here for more kindly disposed Pharisees (as in Luke 13: 31) or for praise for a Jewish scribe (as in Mark 12: 34). The author is thinking of a later time, when excommunication was the punishment for any Jew who acknowledged belief in Jesus (9: 22) and the bitter arguments between Jesus and 'the Jews' reflect not the conditions in Palestine in the time of Jesus but the controversies with the Jews which the Christians had towards the end of the century.

The writer retaliates on the Jews for their opposition to the Church, by putting the blame for the crucifixion on them. It was their perverseness which made them deliver him to Pilate and secured his condemnation (18: 30–40); it was their 'law' which demanded the death penalty (19: 7); they are even prepared to exert political pressure to secure his execution (19: 16). The first 'sign' in the Gospel (2: 1–11—the miracle at Cana, which is full of difficulties if treated as an historical incident) is probably intended to be a symbolic portrayal of the way in which Jesus is able to turn the tasteless water of Judaism (2: 6) into the rich wine of Christianity.

In this way the author sought to present the message to his own contemporaries. We must not, however, accuse him of dishonestly trying to pass off his own views by attributing them to Jesus. Much of his writing admittedly reflects the theology of the early Church rather than the teaching of Jesus in Galilee or Jerusalem. But he believed that the 'Spirit of truth' had led him and he endeavoured thus to give the help which Jesus would afford to those of his own day who were in need and difficulty. Above all, his primary aim was evangelical; he wrote that men might 'believe' and might thereby have 'life in his name' (20: 21).

The Date of the Book

The Gospel was obviously written after the Synoptics. Both tradition and modern criticism agree on this. The circumstances in which it was written, as analysed above, argue for a date towards the end of the first century. We know that by this time some men were doubting the reality of Jesus' human nature and other forms of error were rife, such as we find combated in 1 John (probably written about the same time as the Gospel).

We must not put the book too far into the second century, for when Tatian, an Assyrian, compiled a harmony of the Gospels about 170, he made use of all four. The papyrus fragment of John's Gospel in the John Rylands Library has been dated by the experts at about 150. This shows that the Gospel was in circulation in Egypt by that time. The usual date assigned to the composition is 95 to 105.

The place of writing is generally assumed to be Ephesus. Early tradition states that the writer lived there and this place was a centre for Jewish philosophical thought such as is reflected in this Gospel. It may be a coincidence that it is at Ephesus that we find mention in the New Testament of the continued influence of John the Baptist (Acts 18: 25; 19: 3). An alternative is Alexandria, where Philo had lived, and where there was a strong colony of educated Jews, as well as a Christian Church which was outstanding in learning and study and might well contain a man capable of writing this book. The discovery of the papyrus fragment of A.D. 150 might be held to support Egypt as the place of writing.

THE AUTHORSHIP OF THE BOOK

From the contents of the Gospel we might well conclude that the writer was a cultured and well-educated Jew, with leanings towards Hellenistic thought as it had been developed in the Judaism of Alexandria. His book is the result of meditation on the Synoptic story and other traditions and an attempt to present the good news in terms acceptable to his contemporaries. He seems to be far removed from the outlook of the original apostles and the situation of the eye-witnesses.

The traditional view, however, has been that the book was written by John the son of Zebedee. This was first asserted by Irenaeus, bishop of Lyons in Gaul, towards the end of the second century. He declared that 'John, the disciple of the Lord, who leaned on his breast, himself set forth the Gospel while dwelling in Ephesus, the city of Asia'. He had known Polycarp of Smyrna, who was himself a disciple of John. Thereafter this was the generally accepted opinion in the Church.

This view used to be supported by a seven-fold chain of evidence, which purported to be deduced from the Gospel itself:

(i) The writer was a Jew. He shows his knowledge of Jewish customs and religious practices. His very hatred of the Jews is that of one of them, indignant that his own people had rejected the Messiah.

(ii) The writer was a Jew of Palestine. He names places and suggests he knew the country well—Cana in Galilee (2: 1; 4: 46), a Bethany beyond Jordan (1: 28—the reading Bethabara in the A.V. is taken from late MSS. where scribes substituted this name).

(iii) He was a Jew of Jerusalem. He mentions little-known places such as Bethesda (5: 2), Siloam (9: 7), Solomon's Porch (10: 23), the brook Kidron (18: 1) and Gabbatha (19: 13) and he knows that Bethany is fifteen furlongs from Jerusalem (11: 18).

(iv) He was an eye-witness. It was presumed that the writer referred to himself as 'he that hath seen' (19: 35). In 21: 24 this 'witness' is identified with the one who 'wrote these things' (21: 24). It was held that the teaching of Jesus at the Supper and the remarks of the disciples could have come only from someone who was present.

(v) He was one of the twelve apostles. If he was present at the Supper, this seems obvious.

(vi) He was the one referred to as 'the disciple whom Jesus loved' and 'the other disciple' (13: 23; 18: 15–16; 19: 26–27; 20: 2–8; 21: 7, 20–24).

(vii) This disciple was John the son of Zebedee and he was consequently the author. He is not mentioned in the Gospel (except incidentally in 21: 2) and he sought to hide and yet to suggest his identity in this way.

CRITICISM OF THE TRADITIONAL VIEW

This chain of evidence, however, is not so strong as it seemed to be.

(i) Christian writers in the early second century quote from the Synoptic Gospels and we have the statement of Papias about the authorship of Mark and the writings of Matthew. But no such statement was made about John and quotations from the book are sparse or entirely missing in the very writers whom we should expect to quote from the work of an apostle. Nobody attributed the work to John before Irenaeus in 180 and it is possible that the tradition may be traced simply to him. It is possible that he was himself confused over Polycarp's words about John. Papias mentions two Johns at Ephesus—the apostle and an 'elder' or 'presbyter'—and men of the same name were often confused by early writers. Irenaeus himself mixed up James the son of Zebedee with James of Jerusalem, the brother of Jesus, and other writers sometimes confused Philip the apostle with Philip the evangelist of the Acts.

There are also traces of a tradition that John, instead of living to an old age at Ephesus, died a martyr's death at an early stage in the Church's history. This would of course rule out John as the author of such a late book; but the evidence is not at all clear and is not accepted by many scholars. But the fact that it exists at all bears witness to the uncertainty about the life of John and his connection with the Gospel.

(ii) There were indeed doubts in a number of places about the authorship—Irenaeus himself does not definitely say that John wrote the Gospel, but that he 'set it forth', and other writers hint that other disciples were associated with him in its composition. The book was a centre of controversy in the early Church and it is extremely unlikely that this would have been the case if it was certain that an apostle wrote it. The tradition also came to attribute to John not only the three Epistles but the book of Revelation, which claims, like the others, to have been written by a 'John'. It is certain that this book was not by the same man as the Gospel; the internal evidence shows that. In the Church's fight against Gnosticism and other forms of heresy, the tendency was to attribute to an apostle books which were in frequent use in defence of the faith.

(iii) The writer was certainly a Jew but the arguments that he knew Palestine and Jerusalem well are not conclusive. We do not know where Cana and Bethany-beyond-Jordan were, so we have no means of testing his statements here. The fact that he mentions places in Jerusalem does not prove much, for Luke, a

K

Gentile, who probably did not visit Jerusalem more than once, mentions Solomon's Porch (Acts 3: 11; 5: 12) and knows that the Mount of Olives is a Sabbath-day's journey from Jerusalem (Acts 1: 12). If the writer of the Gospel were a native of Jerusalem, it would rule out the apostle, who was a Galilaean.

(iv) The author does not claim to be an eye-witness. In 19: 35 a distinction should probably be drawn between the 'witness' and the writer. The statement in 21: 24 is a comment added by the Church leaders, perhaps after the publication of the Gospel; it seeks to establish the beloved disciple as the 'witness' and the one who 'wrote these things', which may mean he 'caused these things to be written'. The fact that they had to state so emphatically that 'we know that his witness is true' shows that there was considerable doubt about it at the time.

(v) The marked differences between the Synoptics and John make it very improbable that an apostle wrote it. Mark's Gospel was said to have the authority of Peter behind it and, as we can see from the use made of it by Luke and Matthew, Mark's 'scheme' and narrative became the accepted account of the course of Jesus' life and work. In some places this Gospel differs in emphasis but in others it definitely contradicts the Synoptic details. Elsewhere the author relies on the narrative of Mark and Luke and it is unlikely that an apostle and eye-witness would make use of these two writings in this way.

(vi) The book makes no claim to be by an apostle and it is unlikely that the author would call himself 'the disciple whom Jesus loved'—that he would select himself for the title of 'Jesus' favourite disciple' (as Moffatt translates the phrase). It is more likely that the writer was a disciple of this man and sought to honour his master by giving him this position in Jesus' fellowship. We are probably correct in seeing John the son of Zebedee as the beloved disciple. But it is an idealised John, not the 'son of thunder' of the Synoptics, and he stands for the true disciple of Jesus who understands his master better than the others. This by itself rules out John as the author of the book.

(vii) The style of writing, the ideas and references to current terms and conceptions, show that the writer was acquainted with contemporary Jewish-Greek thought and was probably a Hellenistic Jew.

This is about the only definite conclusion we can come to. Most English scholars have concluded that the author was the man who wrote the three Epistles attributed to John. He calls himself 'The Elder' at the beginning of 2 and 3 John. The only one of whom we know who was specifically called by such a title, without qualification, is John the Elder of Ephesus, mentioned by Papias. Many have concluded that it was he who wrote the Gospel. Hence the name of John was attached to it, and later Christians assumed that this meant the apostle.

In one way we can say it is a gain not to know who wrote the book. We can study it for its own sake and try to understand it, heedless of who it was who put forward this interpretation of the story of Jesus.

There are three critical problems relating to the structure of the Gospel which must be considered.

Two Suspected Passages

(i) The paragraph about the woman taken in adultery (John 8: 1–11) is omitted in all the most trust-

worthy authorities—both Greek MSS. and translations.
(One MS. puts the paragraph in Luke 21: 38.)
This fact in itself casts doubt on the passage as part
of the Gospel and this doubt is reinforced by the narrative itself. The style and vocabulary are quite unlike
those in the rest of the Gospel. It sounds more like a
Synoptic narrative—we might class it as a Pronouncement-story—and was probably a piece of tradition
which became written into copies of the Fourth Gospel
at an early date. Its contents have every indication
that it is a genuine story about Jesus and we may well
add it to the material, especially from Luke, about
Jesus' dealings with despised and outcast people. But
we cannot quote it as part of the writing of the fourth
evangelist.

(ii) Chapter 21 is often referred to as an appendix
to the Gospel. The book comes to a fitting conclusion
with the last words of chapter 20. Jesus has risen, has
returned to his disciples in Jerusalem, even Thomas
has believed, Jesus has given them his commission
and the Spirit, a blessing is pronounced on later disciples and the author concludes with the statement
that he wrote all this that his readers might have 'life
in his name'. Then the story seems to start all over
again—with the disciples not in Jerusalem but in
Galilee, where, apparently not believing the story of
the resurrection, they go fishing and are surprised to
find Jesus meeting them.

The purpose of the chapter seems to be to record
the reinstatement of Peter after his denial of Jesus and
to correct a misconception about the beloved disciple.
Apparently this man had now died and people were
disturbed because they heard that Jesus had said that
he would not die. The writer explains that Jesus' words

had been misunderstood (21: 23). A further puzzle is the unexplained 'we' that appears in verse 24 and the 'I' in verse 25. The former seems to indicate the Church leaders, who authenticate the record, while the last verse seems like a personal comment by an individual, modelled on 20: 30.

It is not agreed among scholars whether the chapter was written by the author of the Gospel or not. The style and language are much the same as the rest of the book. If the author wrote it, we have support for the view that he was not the beloved disciple, who had apparently died by this time. Verse 24 was added by the Church leaders, to emphasise that this disciple was the 'witness' behind the record. If the whole chapter was by another writer, its purpose remains much the same—to show the reinstatement of Peter, perhaps to bring the narrative into line with the Synoptic tradition of a Galilaean resurrection appearance (Mark 16: 7; Matt. 28: 16) and to authenticate the witness of the beloved disciple and set at rest doubts which had been aroused by his death. The somewhat naïve statement with which the chapter ends is probably a personal remark by the scribe.

THE ORIGINAL ORDER OF THE GOSPEL

In some places the order of events in the Gospel seems to be confused. There are three places in particular where a slight rearrangement makes for better and more logical order.

(i) The paragraph in 3: 31–36 is in the present arrangement a continuation of the words of John the Baptist in verses 27–30. These, however, receive a suitable climax in the words of verse 30—'He must increase, but I must decrease'—and verses 31–36 are much like the words attributed in this Gospel to Jesus himself. If verse 31 follows verse 21, as the continuation of the discourse at the interview with Nicodemus, there is a far better connection. The statement in 4: 1, about Jesus' disciples being more than John's, then also follows naturally from the self-effacing statement of John in 3: 30.

(ii) In chapter 5 Jesus is in Jerusalem. Chapter 6 begins with the statement that Jesus then 'went away to the other side of the sea of Galilee'—a strange geographical indication, since in chapter 5 he has not been on any side of the lake, but seventy-five miles away! Chapter 7 states; 'After these things Jesus walked in Galilee', whereas he has already been there in chapter 6. If chapters 5 and 6 are reversed, there is a more natural connection—Jesus is in Galilee, at Cana (4: 46–54); then he proceeds to the other side of the lake (6: 1) and visits Capernaum (6: 59); then he goes to Jerusalem for a Jewish feast (5: 1) and returns to Galilee for a short visit (7: 1).

(iii) At the Last Supper Jesus says, 'Arise, let us go hence' (14: 31), in the middle of his long discourse. But two further chapters of teaching follow. It is very unlikely that the writer intends us to think of chapters 15–16 as being delivered while the disciples stood or were on their way to Gethsemane. There is a much better order if we read chapters 13, 15, 16, 14, 17. Jesus' statement, 'Arise, let us go hence', is followed by his prayer (chapter 17) and the company then proceed to Gethsemane (18: 1).

Other suggested alterations have been made, but these three are the most noteworthy instances. It is suggested that these dislocations were due to the use of papyrus sheets.   The Christians seem to have favoured the use of separate sheets, rather than the long papyrus roll, and if the Gospel was written in this form it would be quite possible for a sheet or sheets to become misplaced and then get bound up with the other sheets in the wrong order.

EPILOGUE

We have been concerned in this book with the technicalities of literary criticism, as applied to the Gospels, using the methods which are employed in the study of any work of literature. There may be some who feel inclined to question its value. There are those who seem to think that criticism of the Gospels means nothing more than 'taking them to pieces', giving a name to sources and attaching a label to each passage. They may doubt whether it helps us to appreciate the books or to understand their message of good news.

There are, however, definite ways in which our reading of the Gospels may be helped by this critical approach and by the conclusions of modern scholars:

(i) Form Criticism enables us to see the Gospels in the making, to go behind the written narratives and to see the form of the good news before it became enshrined in a book. We can recognise the conditions which governed the transmission of the oral traditions and the safeguards which were applied in the Church. We can almost hear the voices of the preachers, as they told the stories and sometimes added their own comments. We can appreciate the motives which led Mark to collect the oral traditions and to write the first attempt at an ordered narrative of the life of Jesus.

(ii) The discovery of the priority of Mark has increased the value of this Gospel. It is safe to say that never, since the first century, has this Gospel been so much studied as it has within the last fifty years. We can appreciate more than ever, reading Mark as the first Gospel, the especial attraction of this book. When we come to the other two Synoptic Gospels, we can see how their authors, with Mark before them, valued the book as a main source of information and made use of it, each in his own way, to produce their versions of the good news, suited to their particular readers.

(iii) The hypothesis of collections of sayings, like Q, has given the evidence for the teaching of Jesus a wider basis. We find that some parables and sayings were handed down in more than one line of tradition (Mark and Q, or Q and L) and that some incidents similarly were told in more than one account (Mark and Q). There is thus a greater likelihood that such accounts are reliable, for they are vouched for not by one witness only but by two and sometimes three. These witnesses were quite independent of each other and the documents were produced in different parts of the Christian world.

(iv) Source Criticism provides also a criterion by which we may judge the reliability of matter found in the Gospels. By discriminating between the different strata of Gospel material, we can assess the relative value and reliability of each. This enables us to judge the trustworthiness of an incident or saying and to decide between different or conflicting versions. We are often able to separate the first account and see how it has been altered or added to in later tradition. If, for instance, we find that we must discard a peculiarity in Matthew's version of the incident taken from Mark, this throws into greater relief the trustworthiness of the Markan narrative. If we are forced to reject some of the additional matter found in the Fourth Gospel, we go back to the synoptics with increased admiration for their portrait of Jesus.

So we are delivered from what Vincent Taylor calls the 'paralysing fear' that, if we challenge, as a result of our critical study, some of the matter found in the Gospels, we are thereby undermining the whole story. As Taylor points out also, this is the answer to the sceptic who fastens on the most doubtful and most unreliable of the Gospel strata for his attacks on the credibility of the whole story.[1] The main bulk of the matter in the Gospels stands firm and bears all the marks of historicity.

A final word of warning is necessary, particularly to those who are new to this line of approach. We must not imagine that this represents all that there is of value in the study of the New Testament. We have been dealing with traditions, documents, methods of compilation, matters of date and authorship. We have been able only incidentally to touch on the real matter of the Gospels—the things which have caused them to be read and treasured throughout all Christian ages.

We have been like an art critic who looks at a great picture and is concerned to find out and explain how the artist has used his colours and achieved his effects. He helps us in this way to appreciate the technique of the painter and we marvel at his masterly treatment of his materials. We may also compare our work with that of a student of architecture, who examines a great cathedral and identifies the style of the doorways, arches, windows and roof, and suggests a date for each part's construction. He helps us to appreciate the history of

[1] *The Gospels: A Short Introduction*, p. 66.

the cathedral and to gain fresh insight into its construction and to see the relations between the various parts which make up the whole building. But after the critic has dissected the picture or the building, we need to stand back and view it as a whole, to marvel at the total impression which it makes on us and to appreciate the great work in its entirety.

So we must do with the Gospels, after we have discussed their sources and methods of construction, their date and authorship. These matters can be used to enable us to appreciate the art and message of each writer, as he sets out to tell the story of Jesus in his own way. Then we shall be the better enabled to realise the nature of the good news which the four books bring to us.

BOOKS FOR FURTHER READING AND STUDY

There is a vast literature on the composition, language and contents of the Gospels. The books listed here are those which have fairly recently appeared and deal more specifically with the subject-matter of this book. A more general list of books on the contents of the Gospels is given in the author's *Study of the Gospels*.

General :

A. Barr: *A Diagram of Synoptic Relations.*
R. H. Lightfoot: *History and Interpretation in the Gospels.*
A Souter: *The Text and Canon of the New Testament (ed. Williams).*
B. H. Streeter: *The Four Gospels.*
R. V. G. Tasker: *The Nature and Purpose of the Gospels.*
V. Taylor: *The Gospels: A Short Introduction.*

Form Criticism :

M. Dibelius: *From Tradition to Gospel.*
B. S. Easton: *The Gospel before the Gospels.*
E. B. Redlich: *Form Criticism.*
V. Taylor: *The Formation of the Gospel Tradition.*

St. Mark's Gospel :

B. W. Bacon: *The Gospel of Mark.*
A. T. Cadoux: *The Sources of the Second Gospel.*
P. Carrington: *The Primitive Christian Calendar.*
J. M. C. Crum: *St. Mark's Gospel.*
A. Farrer: *A Study in St. Mark.*
H. A. Guy: *The Origin of the Gospel of Mark.*
W. L. Knox: *The Sources of the Synoptic Gospels : St. Mark.*
R. H. Lightfoot: *The Gospel Message of St. Mark.*
A. E. J. Rawlinson: *The Gospel according to St. Mark.*

St. Matthew's Gospel :

    G. D. Kilpatrick: *The Origins of the Gospel according to St. Matthew.*

St. Luke's Gospel :

    H. J. Cadbury: *The Making of Luke-Acts.*
    V. Taylor: *Behind the Third Gospel.*

St. John's Gospel:

    C. H. Dodd: *The Interpretation of the Fourth Gospel.*
    W. F. Howard: *The Fourth Gospel in Recent Criticism and Interpretation.*
    W. F. Howard: *Christianity according to St. John.*
    H. Latimer Jackson: *The Problem of the Fourth Gospel.*
    E. F. Scott: *The Fourth Gospel.*